GAME OF
TWO HEARTS

*My life in football
and beyond*

MARK O'BRIEN
FOREWORD BY NIGEL CLOUGH
WITH JOHN BRINDLEY

First Edition.
First published 2023

Published by:
Morgan Lawrence Publishing Services Limited
Ridge House Annexe
16 Main Ridge West
Boston
Lincolnshire
PE21 6QQ
www.morganlawrence.co.uk
email: info@morganlawrence.co.uk
Company number: 12910264

A CIP catalogue record is available for this book from the British
Library.

Photographs are courtesy of:
Nicola Johns, Newport County Football Club, Julia Urwin,
Southport Football Club, Alex Davidson/Getty Images, Kevin
Barnes - CameraSport via Getty Images, Andy Clarke/Derby County
Football Club, PA Images/Alamy Stock Photo, Action Plus Sports
Images, NurPhoto SRL, UK Sports Pics Ltd, PETER POWELL/EPA-
EFE/Shutterstock, Daniel Youngs/Prosports/Shutterstock.

Cover design by LCgrapix. Cover photos by Nicola Johns and Andy Clarke.

Every effort has been made to trace the copyright. Any oversight will be
rectified in future editions at the earliest opportunity by the publisher.

Printed and bound in Bulgaria
by Pulsio Print.

Contents

INTRODUCTION
BY MARK O'BRIEN

'HELLO, which service do you require, police, fire or ambulance?'

'Ambulance, please, I think I'm having a heart attack!'

Absolutely terrified – heart thumping, no safe place to hide – not my sofa, not even my bed.

Barely three years before, I'd been a professional footballer and the 'local hero'. Newport County were a few minutes away from tumbling out of the Football League when I scored the most unlikely of goals to complete our 'great escape'. It was my first ever Football League goal and I was in dreamland – an athlete seemingly at the height of my powers.

It took counselling to show me that the football-mad lad, given his Derby County debut by Nigel Clough at the age of 16 and the nervous wreck of a young man sending a regular SOS to the NHS, were the one and the same Mark O'Brien.

My life has been a rollercoaster. Shortly after that breakthrough at Derby, my life changed forever. I needed open heart surgery, or I'd die. The operation left me on a ticking clock knowing that it was only a matter of time before I'd go through the same thing again.

When I dialled 999 that night I was suffering from the trauma of undergoing further heart surgery at Leicester's Glenfield Hospital. My football career was over, we were living in a pandemic, and I almost despaired of life itself.

But mine is a positive story. Today in 2023 I've never been happier, am grateful for of all my experiences and hoping that others can benefit from my story.

Read on and I'll explain.

FOREWORD
by NIGEL CLOUGH
Derby County manager 2009-2013

WHEN Mark O'Brien came over from Dublin as a teenager and played in Derby's youth team, the first thing I noted about him was his courage. He was absolutely fearless; doing all the old-fashioned things that defenders do, very unusual for such a young player. Little did I know that courage was nothing compared with what he has shown off the field.

We gave him his first team debut as a substitute at Watford in the last game of the season. He was 16 years old and not many 16-year-olds play in the Championship. That's how highly we rated him. He went on to play an important role for Derby County but, without doubt, save for his heart condition and serious injuries, he would have played a lot more games.

His heart diagnosis when still only 16 was a huge shock. That was completely new for us as a club. We were used to dealing with cruciate ligaments and other injuries, not a life-threatening condition. As a club we did what we could for Mark, but he did a hell of a lot more for himself.

Looking back, it's so important that young players are tested. It saved Mark's life. There's more than enough money in football to test all academy players and it should be done. We've seen tragic incidents of young players collapsing or even passing away from undiagnosed heart conditions and that makes the everyday task of winning football matches very unimportant by comparison.

Mark got himself back into the first team and again it says much about how we trusted him that he was in the starting line-up at Forest. Mark was one of the lads who played a full part when we won 2-1 with ten men, a result that goes down in history against Derby's closest rivals. When Mark was struck down with a knee injury, his attitude never changed. He didn't sulk or look sorry for himself. He always came in with a smile on his face and talked to everyone.

Despite injuries limiting his appearances, Mark feels pleased to have achieved what he did. Scoring that goal to keep Newport County in the Football League was a once-in-a-lifetime experience. And the club has become another football home for him.

I think he is perfect for the new player liaison role. Young people respect him – he is a person of honesty and integrity. Football is lucky to have him as he could do what he does in any field.

Mark speaks very well and people in all walks of life relate to him because of his physical and mental struggles. I only wish that I could understand more of what he says – you'd think that accent would have softened after all these years in England and Wales!

Seriously though, this is a great story. One that I'd advise young footballers and others outside of the game to read.

Particularly during a time of mental health crisis in this country, stories like Mark's are very valuable.

CHAPTER ONE
GLORIOUS DUBLIN AND IRISH PRIDE

NEVER Google Ballyfermot! A partly tongue-in-cheek article labels it the worst part of Dublin and warns against going there.

For me, it's a totally different story. Ballyfermot and our two-bedroomed terraced house, in the family from Dad's youth, is home and always will be.

The people I was brought up with are pure gold and many are still my friends today. Yes, there are rough parts of Ballyfermot but that's misleading – it's always been a community and I wouldn't have wanted to have been born anywhere else.

Everyone knew each other in our street, doors remained unlocked, and neighbours mucked in to help each other out. There was a mass gathering for street football with lads getting a tap on the shoulder to ensure that we joined in. Good exercise and part of our togetherness.

Typically, one of my parents' babysitters, Mick Connor, came out to show off his not inconsiderable football skills. Mick understood his football and still claims that he taught me everything I know.

Relationships formed there were for life. Next door neighbour, Anthony Chubb, is still my best friend. Whenever I visit our 'local', The Pigeon Club, during my trips home, I meet with Dean, Dan, Anto, Sebastian, Eddie and Joey. To them, I'm not Mark, the former footballer, or Mark, who had open heart surgery, but plain Mark. Was always like that and always will be.

My parents were very hard workers, providing my slightly older brother James and I with a really good upbringing. They taught us respect, manners and humility and we enjoyed the ordinary, good things in life – not getting all we wanted but never going without anything we needed, schoolbooks and football boots included. We both owe so much to them for becoming the people we are now. That didn't happen by accident but was the result of all the work and time they put into us. I can honestly say they are the perfect parents.

Dad (John) met Mum (Joan) at a house party. He knew some of her friends, they got chatting and he asked her out. The story goes that she said 'no' at first. Mum lived about eight miles away in Finglas and, not having a car, Dad made a sizeable trip on his bicycle to see her. It was well worthwhile because they have been happily married for around 30 years.

Football runs in the blood. Dad could have moved to England to play, but, unselfishly, decided to stay to look after his mother. Aside from his passion for the game, Dad has worked in telecommunications as an engineer for 40 years.

In those early days, I enjoyed playing with my mates. Football wasn't a potential career until later. We practised headers and volleys, even passing, all the important stuff, and I kicked lumps out of my self-proclaimed mentor. As well as football, I enjoyed skateboarding in the street. It was a great place to grow up. For all the so-called problems, most people had jobs and my friends had their aspirations. Some wanted to be in a band, others wanted to play Gaelic football.

I was lucky to pursue my football dream in England. But my friends never thought that I deserted them – not at all. They remained there for me, and I am still there for them. That's the way it has always been for me in Dublin. Most of my friends have got themselves good jobs and careers and done very well. We've all lived our lives in different ways, but still come together to talk about it over a drink.

In the Republic, Gaelic football is the main sport in some parts with association football being the real thing in others. Like Dad and James, I was a keen Manchester United fan during Sir Alex Ferguson's glory years in charge at Old Trafford. My idol was Roy Keane; he was everything that I liked as a footballer – a leader, angry, loved a strong tackle and totally focused on the game. Also, he was Irish and played for United.

The Model School was only 10 minutes down the road from

our house. It was small, didn't have many pupils, and I loved every minute. My parents took a keen interest in my schooling – a little too keen on occasions!

Mum helped the staff. She enjoyed a sing-along, had a great voice, and didn't let the formality of school put her off. One day in the middle of a class, we clearly heard a female voice singing loudly as she walked up and down the corridors. It was Mum on her way into class to collect our monies for the Credit Union.

Poking her head through the door, the class knew that it was the 'voice'. 'Oh no,' I thought. I don't need this. Not worried, she continued singing and played a joke on me by calling me out: "Mark, has your Mum given you any money for the Credit Union?" Everything was taken in good spirits.

Dad made his mark when I was in my fourth or fifth class and taking part in the Christmas play. Unsurprisingly, it included a lot of musical content, and I was given an upbeat song to sing with my magic wand. When Dad said he was planning to see the play, my answer was: "Please don't!" That could have been embarrassing. Closer to the big day, Dad said he wouldn't be coming down because he was working. Phew, that was close. Standing on the stage, wand in hand and in full voice, I spied Dad in the hallway making his way into the room. I had never felt so shy! Dad started clapping and joining in. He knew how embarrassed I was.

I've told two funny stories but I'm very grateful for the great support my parents gave me at primary school and again when I moved to 'big school', St John's College, only 15 minutes from home.

Again, I loved it there even though I started as a minor part. James had already spent two years there and was known as James O'Brien, the footballer. I was James O'Brien's little brother, never likely to match his talent. James went on to sign for Birmingham City and was once regarded as 'the next Roy Keane'.

I was good enough to be courted by teachers who wanted me in the school team. This started a game of tug-of-war with Dad that I was never likely to win. He didn't want me to risk injury, but instead to focus on football outside school. I wanted to play every game that I could. In hindsight, Dad saw the bigger picture and had my best interests at heart. He looked out for me when I didn't realise what was involved.

Dad's word was law, but I did play for the school once. Again, I was asked to play and, as I'd brought my kit, I said 'yes'. That wasn't a game I talked about afterwards with Dad! He wouldn't have been happy that I strayed from his straight and narrow path when playing regularly in the Republic of Ireland age groups.

I'm proud of how positive an influence Dad, who told me growing up that he was 'the white Pele of Ballyfermot', played in my football development. I joined James at our local club Cherry Orchard when he was in the under 8s. Dad wanted me to go there purely to train but the manager, now long-term friend Thomas 'spud' Murphy, had other ideas. 'Spud' wanted to sign and play me; Dad insisted that I was too young. So, he took me for a full trial a year later when I joined Cherry Orchard for real. I trained twice a week and played games at the weekend.

It wasn't all sport as I did very well academically – in fact, I was regarded as being quite clever, even if all my essays tended to be about football! The idea was to do my Junior Certificate, the Irish version of GCSEs, then to concentrate on my football. Maths, English and Geography were my best subjects and I even enjoyed French.

Sports days were another highlight as I did well in all the events, from the 100m and 200m races, to the penalty shootout and different sports. This showed how competitive I was at a very young age and that I must have some talent.

The Principal's Cup was a very unusual but very good football tournament that I enjoyed at school. All the age groups played each other, so first years faced up to sixth formers. A team of teachers were a target of mine. Whilst I didn't dislike any of the staff, I liked some more than others! So, when I tackled a teacher I didn't get on too well with, it was an early example of my 100 per cent full-bloodied tackle. He couldn't give me a detention because it was part of the game.

Although I loved school, I looked forward to flying away at every opportunity to play in football matches elsewhere. These usually happened at half term or the end of term, and sometimes meant missing a few days of lessons. I was in the top classes for my studies, so this made things harder for me. Some teachers were ok with it as I was playing sport at a high level; others weren't so happy.

Closer to my Junior Certificate, the female religion teacher took me to one side to say that I should give my education my full attention. She didn't think I would make it as a professional footballer and needed something more solid to fall back on.

Her bluntness created some doubt in my mind. I had never considered anything other than football for a living, was doing well with the Republic age groups and convinced that it would happen. What if she was right? Was I in danger of being very disappointed?

I used her words to give me even greater motivation. What did she know? She was a religion rather than a sports teacher, wasn't she? My mission was to prove her wrong. In any case, I did myself proud in my Junior Certificate. I finished with three As – Geography, Religion (ironically) and Maths – with Bs in English and French, Cs in History and Business Studies and a D in science. I had worked hard, but my mind was set on signing for Derby County rather than furthering my education.

Three or four years later, I had the joy of being invited back for a school reunion. Being in Derby's first team was a talking point with my mates and a certain religion teacher. To her credit, she had seen how well I was doing. She was a Leeds United supporter and I'd been part of a team who had just beaten her favourites. Talk about proving her wrong – and rubbing it in!

To be honest, I don't have anything against her at all. She had my best interests at heart in urging me not to neglect my education which does happen in the lives of many youngsters whose football dream bites the dust. So, yes, I understood what she said and why she said it and am grateful she spurred me on.

I've already hinted at it, but James was better than me. Better technically and better potentially as a player. I did everything possible though to emulate him. He captained Dublin in the Kennedy Cup, in which youngsters in the different regions got together when we were aged 11 and 12, and a couple of years later so did I. It was great to lead that team to victory and what a side it was, including Jeff Hendrick, Robbie Brady and Matt Doherty, who all went on to play in the Premier League and represent the Republic of Ireland at senior level.

'Spud' was a very big influence on me as a person and as a footballer and it was great that I grew up having the same club manager for about 10 years. 'Spud' gave me a taste of what a real manager was all about. No matter how youthful we were, if we fell below expectations, he let us know. Thanks to him, I grasped something of the grit, determination and never-say-die mentality that a footballer needs.

Dad was a major influence on both brothers. He knew his football and our capabilities. Like Spud, he didn't shy away from telling us when we failed to fulfil them. He also put me right when I took an interest in the different coloured boots that other players were wearing. I wanted to wear yellow or pink boots, but Dad insisted that wasn't the way. "Have you ever seen a defender wear anything other than black?" he asked. I hadn't. "You don't want to be flashy. You need to do your job," he added. That meant kicking, heading, tackling and reading the game.

He cited the example of former Manchester United star Paul McGrath, one of the outstanding players in Jack Charlton's Republic of Ireland side. McGrath never had real pace but was rarely caught out because he was always one step ahead of the rest. That taught me a lot as a defender. Dad also spoke of the importance of going into a tackle full bloodied like McGrath. When you try to protect yourself, you are more likely to be injured. I played like McGrath – never seeking to hurt an opponent but going in 100 per cent to win the ball.

The pattern of following in my brother's shoes continued as we went through the Republic of Ireland age groups. It was my number one ambition to pull on a senior green shirt, represent my country at the highest level and also to make my parents proud. It remains my one regret from my football career that never happened. Watching former young teammates and friends Robbie Brady and Jeff Hendrick was the closest I got.

Nothing matches the pride of singing the national anthem alongside your teammates, then representing your country – particularly such a passionate nation as Ireland. That was one of my main motivations to become a professional footballer. I am very proud to have captained the Republic at under 15s, 16s and 17s and been picked at under 19 and under 21 level, although injury prevented me from playing.

I grew up with international football even though I was too late to enjoy the Jack Charlton era. The way that the community comes together to support and celebrate the national team is fantastic. An Englishman with a 1966 World Cup winners' medal, Big Jack embraced Irish culture – one of the reasons for his success. He had very good footballers, but played in a way that he thought would be most successful. Mostly the ball was knocked up to a big man up front to hassle the opposition into mistakes and get us further up the pitch.

I was only four years old when the Republic reached the quarter finals of the World Cup in America in 1994, so remember our adventures under Mick McCarthy more clearly. The 2002 World Cup in South Korea and Japan left a lasting impression. Many games were played during lesson time, but we were allowed to follow the action on TV.

This was the World Cup where the manager and Roy Keane fell out big time on the eve of the tournament. Fortunately, that didn't stop the team and the country having a great time. I stayed at home for the Cameroon game that kicked off at about 9am. The excitement when Matt Holland scored the winning goal was unforgettable. It all boiled down to Germany when we needed a draw to reach the knockout stages. We were a goal down and heading out before Robbie Keane nodded a 90th minute equaliser and the country went ballistic. I remember car drivers beeping their horns and people hugging each other!

Fast forward a few years to Martin O'Neill's side at the Euros in 2010; there was a very special moment when Robbie Brady headed a late winner against mighty Italy to send us through to the knockout stages. Experiences like that – and watching other big internationals at the Euros in the pub – were what I wanted to emulate on the pitch.

James was the first O'Brien to make it as a professional. After signing a three-year deal with Brum, he played for Bradford City before quitting England and coming back home where he represented St Patrick's, Shelbourne, Athlone Town and Bohemians. Today he works in a 'normal' job and I think he regrets pulling back on his dream. That ultimately was the difference between the two brothers. I wasn't as talented but refused to take 'no' for an answer. James wanted instant success. I was patient, prepared to wait years, but refused to accept failure.

One of my early teammates was Jeff Hendrick, later a friend

and colleague at Derby. I knew Jeff from the age of 10 or 11 when we played together in the Foyle Cup in Northern Ireland for St Kevin's Boys. It was there that another first occurred when I was sick on the bus travelling up with the lads. This was very embarrassing, but it then happened every time before a match and almost became a ritual. I got myself worked up and anxious before kick-off and that was a way of releasing the tension. I warmed up on the pitch, then returned to the dressing room to vomit. I would have thought something was wrong if I wasn't sick.

Whilst playing for the Republic's under 14 and under 15s, I went for trials with Manchester City, Liverpool and Blackburn Rovers. Winning the Republic of Ireland under 16 player of the year award was a special achievement for me but in one way nothing new. In fact, it was a family tradition, starting with my cousin Clifford Byrne, who had a very good professional career in England, and James a couple of years before me.

Starting at Sunderland, Clifford played almost 300 times for Scunthorpe United during successful years when they were promoted to the Championship and more recently was Grant McCann's assistant at both Doncaster Rovers and Hull City, He was well placed to offer advice when I got the chance to come to England, saying that it was one thing to do so, but much harder to stay there. He encouraged me to keep my standards high and work hard.

I played in a very good Republic side managed by Vincent Butler and was very proud to take the role of captain. One very memorable international took us across the border to face Northern Ireland where we came back from a goal down before I grabbed the winner. So, I can always say that I was an international goalscorer, even if it was only the once.

Of the three interested clubs, I fancied Blackburn and wanted to sign for them. City's academy was so big that I felt like a number and there was never going to be a place for me. It was much the same at Liverpool, although both were good experiences. Blackburn academy coach Gary Bowyer was keen to sign me, saying there was a contract on the table.

But fate took over and Derby County made their move. At first, they weren't confident that I would agree to join them, but invited me to Liverpool on a Saturday to play against Everton Under 14s. Getting off the plane, I met my teammates for the first time in the dressing room before the game and my big day went very well. We won the match 3-2 and I got the winner. Derby were impressed with what they saw and invited me over from Dublin for a week to train with them.

I was 14 and the academy manager asked me after my first training session if I realised who I was training with. I thought it was my age group, but I'd been with the under 17s and 18s without looking out of place. Providing I did well, he was sure there'd be something for me at the end of the week.

I kept myself to myself but loved the whole atmosphere around the club. It was a massive thing for me, a teenager who had flown over from Ireland, to find a place that felt like home. I had no hesitation signing a pre-contact at Derby where I started training with the under 16s before moving up to the under 18s when I turned 16.

CHAPTER TWO
BREAKTHROUGH AND HEARTBREAK ONE AT DERBY

I KNEW very little about Derby County's famous history or even the great Brian Clough! Coverage of the English league clubs was fairly limited in Ireland during my upbringing. We heard plenty about Manchester United and Liverpool and that was about it.

The Rams won the old First Division title twice in the 1970s, under Clough and then Dave Mackay, and reached the semi final of the European Cup before going out in very controversial circumstances to Juventus.

Yet I got a ribbing from friends because, whilst I was on trial at Pride Park, the Rams were creating history of a far different kind. Promoted through the Championship play offs, they won only 11 points in the Premier League under first, Billy Davies and then, Paul Jewell. But joining 'the worst team in Premier League history' was no problem to me. I was delighted to be there.

I didn't have much contact with Davies. He had a squad of about 35 to 40 players, including some on extremely high wages, which made it much more difficult to develop a bond between the players.

And I didn't have much of a relationship either with Paul Jewell, who was charged with the near impossible task of keeping Derby in the Premier League, then rebuilding back in the Championship. This was very hard because the whole club needed to readjust and that meant moving players on. There was an air of uncertainty about the place and he was dealing with lads on big money with big egos.

I trained every day of the week, except for Thursday when

I went to college, and played football at the weekend. I loved every minute of it. Naturally I was miles away from the first team, but it was a nice touch when Paul Jewell wished me a happy birthday when I turned 16. That told me I was known about the place.

With the club still struggling to get back onto its feet after relegation, Jewell was sacked on the eve of our remarkable 1-0 victory over mighty Manchester United in the first leg of the League Cup semi final, and Nigel Clough came in as manager. Again, I probably didn't take in what an historic move this was. Brian Clough was talked about more by the older lads in the squad who noted the similarities and differences between father and son.

To me, Nigel Clough was a top manager. I'll go into more detail later about how he backed and encouraged me when I was at my lowest ebb with my heart condition, and I will always be grateful for his support. He always had your back, if he liked you. That didn't mean he wouldn't be on your case – perhaps even more so. But everything he did and said was with a view to making better footballers and better human beings.

Whilst I was playing for the under 18s, Nigel Clough looked at me and gave me a chance for the reserves against Glenn Hoddle's academy side. Our second team largely consisted of first and second year scholars and I was still a schoolboy. I was on the bench as one of the senior scholars was injured.

I got on as centre back for the last seven minutes and immediately flung myself into tackles and made a couple of blocks. Nigel Clough liked what he saw and said I'd done really well. That got me into the next youth squad, and I was taking things in my stride. So much so that I was picked to play in the reserve side in a cup final at home to Sunderland at Pride Park. There were some big names in the Rams side, such as Roy Carroll and Jeff Hendrick, whilst Martyn Waghorn, who later became a Derby favourite, was up front for the Black Cats.

I don't remember too much about the game and nothing of the last 10 minutes. That was after the ball was played down the channel and, trying to nod the ball out of play, I ended up headbutting the Sunderland striker and collapsing in a heap. The boss asked if I intended to headbutt him and said 'good lad' when I answered yes. I didn't know what I was saying but the manager interpreted it that I had no problem putting my head where others feared to put their feet. Nigel Clough said: "I would tackle my Nan if she had the ball – that's the kind of player Mark was."

One of the unwritten rules around the club was to obey first teamers when they asked you to do something. Robbie Savage, Welsh international, ultra-competitive midfielder and now a football pundit, was one of the first to test me out. "OB, two sugars!" he said. And he wasn't impressed with my tea. "That's only half a cup," he said, insisting that I put it right. Sav took an interest in me from day one and was one of the first players who had my back. I was thoroughly enjoying myself and it was changing me as a person. Still quiet off the pitch. I was becoming a different character on it, giving instructions and encouragement to my teammates.

I expected to go back home at the end of the youth team's season, but that changed after Mum and Dad chatted to Nigel Clough after the first team secured our Championship status in our last home game with a 1-0 victory over Charlton Athletic. The final match against Watford at Vicarage Road now had nothing riding on it and I was more interested in the final academy fixture.

"See you next week," Dad said. "Don't worry about that, I'll be back home soon," I answered. But, no, he was insistent that his 'mate' Nigel wanted me for the first team. I thought Dad was joking. Even when coach Gary Crosby said on the Monday: "OB, you are with the first team today!" the penny didn't drop.

It was an 'oh my God' moment going onto the training pitch, alongside the likes of Miles Addison, Robbie Savage, Roy Carroll, Stephen Bywater, Giles Barnes, Rob Hulse and Barry Bannon. Nerves and shyness were put to one side once we started playing. Once over that white line, I got stuck in and had no problem making myself heard.

My academy mates wanted to know how I got on and it was very kind of some of the first teamers to say that, had there been a man of the match for the training session, it would have been me. I trained with the first team until the Thursday when Nigel Clough asked what I thought about the weekend. I thought he meant the academy game, but he was talking about Watford. I was on the bench!

I couldn't believe it. Dad had been telling the truth after all and I was getting my first taste of first team football. I reverted to my normal off-the-pitch self by keeping very quiet on the coach as we travelled down to London on the Saturday and was understandably very nervous. Eventually we got the stadium, I took part in our warmup and sat myself down on the bench. Then came another surprise.

Second year scholar and fellow substitute Mark Dudley looked over assistant manager Andy Garner's shoulder and said that I was coming on after 60 minutes! Our experimental line up was 3-0 down at half time and, as I looked at the stadium clock, I saw it read 57, then 58 minutes. I jogged gently down the touchline, stretching my hamstring once and putting on my shin pads. Not much of a warmup, but that was all I knew.

I'd only ever played in front of a couple of hundred people before. I was nervous and anxious but beginning to enjoy the atmosphere, even though the vast majority of the 22,000 fans were against us. I'll always remember Nigel Clough's instructions. "Kick it and head it, you're a defender." Simple as that.

I came on for Lewin Nyatanga and played alongside Rob Hulse, usually a striker, who'd bagged the winning goal against Charlton the week before. "You're the centre half, you tell me what to do!" he said. I made several challenges on the deck and in the air and cleared one effort of the line as we eventually lost 3-1.

True to form, whenever I did something positive, Robbie Savage was first to pat me on the back and say, 'well done'. He did a lot to bring out my confidence. Losing was disappointing, but at least we didn't concede whilst I was on the pitch and the lads were very good to me afterwards saying I had done my job well.

I was among the top three youngest Derby players when I made my debut – and am still in the top five. My exact age was 16 years, 5 months and 13 days. Mum and Dad were both there to watch and were delighted. The whole thing was surreal. The previous summer I'd been playing for Cherry Orchard in the Dublin League; now I'd just made my first team debut for one of England's most famous clubs.

I loved every minute and felt that I'd arrived. After getting a taste of an occasion such as that, I wanted more. If only the season was starting rather than ending!

Instead, my life took a completely different turn. Legendary Liverpool manager Bill Shankly famously said: "Football isn't a matter of life and death. I am very disappointed with that attitude. I can assure it's much, much more important than that." For me, that's literally true. Being a young professional footballer probably saved my life!

I had no reason to think that I had a health problem. I'd always been fit and healthy. I was Derby's academy scholar of the year and had now made my first team debut. What could possibly be wrong?

Like the other Derby players, I had six weeks off. That 'holiday' meant going home to Dublin and settling back into life as normal. It was great when family and friends congratulated me on making my debut, but I was more than happy kicking a ball in the street and behaving like a typical teenager. I was sent a pre-season pack from the club with guidelines to ensure that I was fit when we returned in July. This meant going to the gym, swimming and running. I didn't know how vital this was to prepare for the rigours of pre-season training but had no problem with it. All I wanted was to kick on with my new career.

Back in Derby, we wore heart monitors in training. Normal routine stuff to measure if players are putting in the necessary hard work. I'd never seen one before nor had my heart rate checked. There had never been a need.

When my heart rate was a fair bit higher than the others, it was thought that this reflected well on my efforts. Joining my teammates for our health screening, I wasn't in the least bit worried. We lined up one by one with academy physio, Neil Sullivan, before undergoing an ECG (electrocardiogram). The whole thing lasted between 20 and 30 minutes and I presumed it was a formality.

The checks looked at our heart valves, ventricles and vessels and I was surprised when told to wait behind for a second. The door was shut and the specialist said the tests had shown up a small defect. One of my valves was leaking – nothing to worry about, but they would keep an eye on it.

Asked if I ever felt dizzy or breathless, I answered very

honestly I was perfectly fine. Told I would need an operation in 50 or 60 years, my reaction was positive – this wouldn't affect my football. Neither I nor the club told my parents about the finding. There was nothing to tell. It was a matter between the specialist, physio, fellow staff and me.

I went back into training as normal and sat in the spa bath after one session when fitness coach, Steve Haines, looked at the heart monitors. Maximum and average readings were 180 and 150; mine were significantly higher at 218 and 202. The physios and other staff hadn't encountered this before and thought it needed to be followed up. So, an MRI scan was booked at Leicester's Glenfield Hospital a few weeks after the initial diagnosis.

The specialist said my aorta heart valve was leaking and, on a scale from one to ten in terms of seriousness, he'd give it a seven or eight. I didn't understand what that meant. He referred me to another specialist because the condition had progressed since first noticed. This time I told Dad everything providing he didn't tell Mum because she is a born worrier.

A groin problem that kept me out of training before my next appointment turned out to be a blessing in disguise. That meant my heart rate wasn't monitored for a couple of weeks and I avoided putting more strain on it. The second specialist agreed that my condition had progressed and estimated I'd need operating on in 20 to 30 years. Again, I was relieved this wouldn't stop me playing the game I love. He insisted on me seeing a surgeon for his professional opinion – an appointment that I attended with the club physio and my parents.

During this time, the club didn't release any information on my condition. In any case, I wasn't well known enough for fans to be wondering why I wasn't being mentioned as a possible first team player.

I remember almost word for word what the surgeon said. We were sat in a little room when he came in carrying a model of the human heart. He explained that I had a bicuspid valve. Each valve has three cusps but only two of mine were working – the other was faulty, allowing blood back into my heart. My heart was now THREE times as big as it should have been and working twice as hard to function properly. The surgeon's message was stark and blunt: I needed an operation quickly or I was going to die!

My extreme physical fitness prevented me from suffering dizziness, drowsiness and fatigue. But walking up a flight of stairs could be the last thing I did. That was truly shocking. The surgeon looked in his diary and noted that he had a free date in two weeks. Almost in the blinking of an eye, 60 years had been whittled down to a mere fortnight and I was booked for open heart surgery!

Those words almost floated above my head. It all felt so unreal, like he was talking to someone else. Not me. This sort of thing happens to much older people, not a teenager who had just made his first team debut. When was this nightmare going to stop?

I had three choices – replace the leaky valve, with either a pig's valve or a metallic one, or swap it for a lung valve. The main thing on my mind wasn't life or death but which option was better for my football? "You'll be lucky to kick a ball with your mates, let alone play professionally," he said.

My answer to the question, though, was the pig's valve. So that was the one for me. The surgeon had a warning – there was no guarantee that it would give me what I wanted and I shouldn't be too disheartened if I never played again. Also, the pig valve would last a maximum of five years whereas the metallic version was for life. I can hardly believe how naïve I was in risking my future for an outside chance to play football. But, at the time, it was a no brainer. I was so excited about what had happened so far, I desperately wanted more.

Throughout this drama, Derby County and Nigel Clough supported me fully. Knowing a huge question mark hung over my head, he gave me a three-and-a-half-year deal, ensuring that I was well looked after as I fought to get back on my football feet. They say everything happens for a reason and there were more than footballing reasons why I went to Pride Park. They were the right people for me when I needed them most. They looked after me as one of their own.

Nigel Clough told me to go home to Dublin to spend time with my family before the operation. That was the right thing for me. My parents did everything they could to fill me with confidence that I would be alright – I didn't smoke or drink and was very fit, making me the perfect patient, they said.

My operation took place at Glenfield, in Leicester, a hospital renowned for its heart care, and lasted six and a half hours. Now it was up to me. Despite the surgeon's words, I never doubted that I could get back on the football field.

The news was made public to the fans with the *Derby Telegraph* reporting on November 4, 2009, 'Rams academy ace O'Brien has heart surgery.' This gave me the chance to say I was feeling fit and healthy and looking forward to playing football again. The report added 'he faces three to four months rest before he will look to resume his promising career'.

I was back at the Moor Farm training ground within days mixing with my academy mates. My reaction to a very traumatic time in my young life was praised by Rams youth team manager, John Perkins, who described me as a 'very calm individual who takes everything in his stride and this has been no different. He is an extremely dedicated professional who looks after himself and there is no doubt when he gets back into training, he will be working hard to get back to the level he was at before and hopefully even better.'

Nigel Clough phoned to ask how I was getting on with my walking rehab, and how Mum and Dad were. I was away from the club for around three months but never out of their minds. I returned to Derby in the January. Football clubs are used to rehabilitating players with injuries, but how do you help someone back from a heart problem? This was seriously new territory for them as well as me.

At first it was light jogging with fitness coach Steve Haynes as my constant companion. This was very low-level fitness work and I was given a heart monitor to ensure that all was ok. This was my way of life for three or four months. I returned properly to training in April. By then, fans knew of my problems and I received a lot of support, both on social media and at the club where Neil Sullivan, Steve Haynes and the Derby physios were all amazing.

Eventually I was fit enough to take part in an in-house reserve game and was on the pitch for the full 95 minutes. That was an important step on the road back. Then I was picked for the youth team to play against Manchester United at Old Trafford. As the game was broadcast on *MUTV*, Dad watched live as I got another 90 minutes under my belt. Apparently, he saw me make a few interventions in the air and on the ground before delightedly telling Mum that I was alright.

It was a great feeling to be involved again with the first team as we rounded off a stuttering Championship season with a 2-0 victory over Cardiff City at Pride Park after an incredibly difficult year for me. I was on the bench alongside fellow youngsters, Jeff Hendrick and Ryan Connelly, and didn't get onto the pitch. But the feeling of being in the squad again was a big lift.

Things progressed from there and I found myself playing in every pre-season friendly as Nigel Clough's team warmed up for the 2011/2012 season. The in-house joke was that I was always last in training runs because of my heart. But I told the manager it was because I wasn't a very good runner. He appreciated that and said running wasn't the be all and end all and that I was proving my fitness by taking part in all the games.

I got my chance for what turned out to be my longest spell in the Rams side because of an injury to defender Russell Anderson on the opening day of the season against Birmingham City at Pride Park.

I was on the bench when Russell pulled his hamstring with the score at 1-1 and made my home debut in a lively game we eventually won 2-1. I felt I'd done well and was delighted to be in the starting line up three days later for the League Cup tie at home to Shrewsbury Town. That was a night when I was brought instantly back down to earth.

We were expected to progress against a side two divisions below us even with a much changed team. But it didn't work out that way as we were 3-0 down by half time and I made a bad mistake allowing James Collins, more recently a Derby striker, to score. Although we got two goals back in the second half, we were on the wrong end of a giant killing and I wouldn't have been surprised had I been dropped.

Instead, the manager gave me a first league start at Vicarage Road on the Saturday. It was quite an occasion for me to go back to where my Derby first team career had begun before the heart surgery. And this time it was a happy outcome as I helped us to keep a clean sheet and a Steve Davies goal enabled us to win 1-0. That was an amazing feeling for me.

I was playing alongside Jason Shackell, a partnership that had a lot going for it. He was a natural left sided centre back whilst I played on the right. As the more experienced player, he helped me out a lot and encouraged me as much as he could.

The formula worked again at Blackpool where we made it three league wins out of three with another hard-earned 1-0 success. When we defeated Doncaster Rovers 3-0 at Pride Park, they tell me it was Derby's best start to a season for 106 years! For my part, I was thrilled to be part of it and enjoying every second.

Victory over out-of-form Burnley at Pride Park would have taken us into the first international break on top of the Championship. Instead, it was a time for me to learn a very important lesson.

The game was going ok in the first half when a long ball was played over the top with Burnley striker Charlie Austin chasing me. Instead of doing the simple thing and clearing the ball, I flicked it over my head to Jason Shackell. It was the sort of moment that drew applause from the fans after they realised my trick had worked, but Nigel Clough was furious. He asked what the hell I thought I was doing at half time and I couldn't give him an answer. That was very unlike me and I had no idea why I did it.

It got worse in the second half when, again instead of clearing the ball, I saw an intended pass to left back Gareth Roberts cut out and the ball was crossed for Austin to put them in front. Theo Robinson equalised with 19 minutes left but they finished the stronger and Austin scored the winner.

Nigel Clough did me a favour afterwards with his post-match words, saying that it was the kind of thing that happens with inexperienced players. But he let me know what he thought during the week when he joined in one of our training sessions. He was jogging towards me to challenge for a ball near the touchline and this time I booted the ball about three pitches away. "Now you're learning," he said. The important thing was not to repeat the same mistakes.

The learning curve was only just beginning. I'd been naïve

enough to believe that, if I did my job properly, I had nothing to fear from any striker. Playing against Lukas Jutkiewicz at Coventry showed me that there's more to football than that. He was a clever striker who knew his game a lot better than I did. I couldn't get close to him on the deck or dominate him in the air. Usually, I fancied myself to win the aerial battle, but he timed his jumps better to get the flick ons.

The game largely passed me by as Coventry overcame their poor start to the season to beat us 2-0, but I came away from there knowing I needed to adjust the way I played depending on whom I was up against.

Then came 'the big one'. I was beginning to realise that it didn't matter too much how well we had started the season, the East Midlands derby against our closest rivals Nottingham Forest at the City Ground was the game that really mattered for many supporters. I must admit I had no idea of the intensity of the rivalry between the two clubs until I experienced it for myself.

Nigel Clough did his best to prepare us for what is always a very special, hostile atmosphere. Naturally he knew all about Forest and Derby, clubs that both enjoyed their most successful ever time under the management of his dad and Peter Taylor. Then he was a top player at Forest, becoming one of their top goalscorers and winning full England caps. Rumour has it that he once scored twice for Forest in a victory over The Rams at the City Ground. Now he was going back there in charge of 'the enemy' and he let us know in no uncertain terms what we would be up against.

Fans and players alike would both be right up for the match, he said, and Forest were likely to make a very quick start on their own pitch as they had done in a couple of our recent trips to Trentside. This message began to sink in as our coach approached the ground and we witnessed the aggression and hatred of Forest supporters. I'm not having a go at them or Forest as a club. I prefer to see it as a football occasion, and this is one of the biggest rivalries in the country.

To make things even more tasty, Forest had recently appointed former Derby assistant manager and England boss Steve McClaren to the City Ground hot seat with the expectation that they would push for promotion. They had made a disappointing start but were no doubt looking for a win against their closest rivals to kick start their season. We were not so strongly fancied – at least outside of Derby – but had followed up our opening day win over Brum with three more league successes before going into the Forest match on the back of a couple of defeats.

Some people freeze in such a hostile environment where there is literally hatred being projected your way from the stands, others thrive on it. I was naturally the latter. I loved it. After facing up to the wiles of Jutkiewicz at Coventry, I was expecting a more predictable but very physical battle with Forest's newly signed striker Ishmael Miller – and I wasn't disappointed.

Although Nigel Clough prepared us for a quick start, what happened in almost the first attack of the match completely threw us out of our stride. Miller was involved as he was bundled over by our goalkeeper Frank Fielding, causing a double whammy. Not only did referee Scott Mathieson point to the penalty spot but Fielding was also shown a straight red card.

We needed to think clearly. Fortunately, we had a second goalkeeper on the bench in Adam Lagzdins and the player sacrificed was forward Tomasz Cywka. This meant a potentially lonely battle up front for Theo Robinson.

We were still in shock when Andy Reid rolled the ball into the corner of the net past substitute goalkeeper, Adam Legzdins, to give Forest an early lead. That gave Forest a major advantage and got the home crowd even more strongly behind them. In circumstances like that, you can do one of two things – collapse and get turned over, or fight. There was never any doubt what we would do. First, it was important not to concede a second goal. Weathering the early storm meant that we could work ourselves back into the game and that's what we did.

I was involved in the controversy around Jamie Ward's fantastic opening goal for Derby although I didn't do anything. I was the nearest player to Forest's Chris Cohen when he was injured. Jeff Hendrick took him on and, as Cohen turned to attempt to close him down, his knee collapsed under him and he fell awkwardly. It wasn't a foul and nobody had any idea that he was so badly injured. The home fans howled for the game to stop, particularly as Wardy picked up possession in space and was making his way towards the edge of their penalty area.

Call me biased, if you like, but the referee made the right decision. There was no reason to stop play and time seemed to stand still as Wardy tormented the home defence before sticking the ball past Lee Camp. That was 1-1 with about 30 minutes gone and reason to believe that our ten men could do something after all.

It certainly gave Nigel Clough a different half time talk and McClaren and co something to chew on. Again, we knew Forest would come at us after the break to try to restore their lead, but this time there were no dramas. In fact, we should have gone in front when Jeff Hendrick, nodded wide from a couple of yards. Had we missed our big chance?

No! Midway through the second half came a goal that Derby fans will never forget. I played a part, lobbing the ball forward for Ben Davies to touch aside to Hendrick 20 yards out and he arrowed a low shot into the Bridgford End net. Amazingly, we were 2-1 in front. Our fans were going crazy whilst the atmosphere in the ground was now very different. Away teams are always aware that when things start to go against the home side, the fans get restless. And Forest supporters were beginning to turn on their side.

We needed to avoid giving them or Forest any encouragement. The rest of the game was a blur as Forest mounted a late siege, but I was in a good rhythm making clearances, getting in tackles and generally putting my body on the line – all things that I loved to do as a defender. The result was that, despite their pressure, Forest weren't able to create any clear chances.

I'll never forget the feeling at the final whistle. There we were jumping around and celebrating with our fans, almost in a state of shock. I knew that I'd had a good game but that was a team victory if ever there was one. Everyone contributed from the replacement goalkeeper to Theo Robinson up front – I swear he worked his socks off, coming off the pitch drenched in sweat, having put in the ultimate shift for his team. As a defender, it gives you a big lift when your striker acts as the first line of defence to make things more difficult for the opposition.

We felt we got what we deserved at the City Ground and

were still on a massive high as the coach left the stadium. As we passed a pub, there were a few bangs on the horn to alert Forest fans who responded by throwing glasses and cups at us. In that moment, we weren't that bothered. It just emphasised that we had achieved something special.

That victory at Forest is still commented upon by Rams' fans more than a decade later and it was wonderful to be part of it. It was one of the highlights of my professional career and created great memories, which is what ultimately football is all about.

Seven days later we were still buzzing as I played another 90 minutes in a 3-0 home victory over Millwall that took us up to third place in the Championship. A genuine promotion challenge seemed on the cards.

After playing in a 1-1 draw against Barnsley, I was given another reality check at Leicester where I found David Nugent and Darius Vassell as much of a handful as Jutkiewicz and more. Things were ok in the first half when I earned a big cheer from Nigel Clough for going in for a full bloodied 50-50 with renowned hard man Paul Konchesky and sending the former England defender flying over my back. The big man liked that.

As at Coventry, the two lads up front were clever and difficult to read. They varied coming short or long and their movement was quick and elusive in the box. Let's just say I struggled and the 4-0 defeat was the worst I'd suffered as a first team player.

Adam Le Fondre was another very tough opponent – a fox in the box who was difficult to pick up – but at least we had the consolation of getting a point from a 2-2 draw at Reading.

I then suffered a temporary setback jumping for a header in the opening stages of the clash with Portsmouth. I landed on my shoulder and couldn't lift my arm above my head. It was thought I'd strained ligaments in my shoulder but, fortunately, I was only out for a week.

Nigel Clough welcomed me back as my shoulder was being strapped before the visit to Peterborough but that would have been a good game to miss!

It started well enough with us going 2-0 up in the first half and me grabbing a rare assist. The ball was played to the far post where I knocked it back across for Theo Robinson to net our first goal. They say 2-0 leads are never safe and it's amazing how a game can change when the other side get a goal back. In this case, that goal came early in the second half and suddenly we were defending and defending.

Eventually Posh drew level and, with the momentum in the home side's favour, we were holding on for a point. Even that proved beyond us as, in the 94th minute, we failed to fully clear a corner and Grant McCann caught it on the volley and sent it flashing through a queue of bodies and into the bottom corner.

I still remember dropping to my knees in despair. I always took losing and conceding goals very personally and, on this occasion, I was very upset about being in a defence that had shipped three in one half of football.

I had done enough in my extended stint in the first team to win praise from Nigel Clough, but the recovery of first choice defender Shaun Barker from injury changed my season. Nigel explained it to me as well as he could. I'd probably played more games than I had expected and merited my place, he said, but Barker was his key man and needed to play. I accepted his comments and chose to bide my time.

That opportunity should have come on Boxing Day when we played Leeds United. Nigel told me in training that he was going to bring me back in before I suffered a freak injury in training. When the ball was played to me, I slipped and hurt my knee without knowing the significance of it. The initial pain had gone but the physio looked and said I had injured my cruciate ligaments. "How long will I be out for – a couple of weeks?" I said naively. "No, that's you done for the season!"

That was another hammer blow – this time a real football injury. Best I could do though was to believe that, having recovered from open heart surgery, this wasn't going to beat me. However, there was a feeling of helplessness about this. In some ways, it hit me even harder than the heart condition. It's strange but I could almost take my football career being ended by something outside my control – the heart condition – but not an injury that I thought I could have avoided.

Again, I was indebted hugely to Neil Sullivan and Steve Haynes who both helped me hugely. Their attitude was to try to make a positive out of a negative by seeing what they could do to improve me physically for when I came back. It's relevant here to remember that I was still only 18 years old and not fully physically developed. I was competing in a man's game and it made sense to try to bulk me up.

At first, I was on crutches, then had to wear a knee brace for 15 weeks. This was mentally very, very tough. Instead of feeling sorry for myself, I worked very hard in the gym where I began the hard physical work. Neil and Steve drew up a plan for me combining a calorie-rich diet with gym work. In addition, teammates Jeff Hendrick and Ryan Connolly drove me here, there and everywhere and were generally there when I needed help.

In one sense, I was frustrated because I knew my football career may not be very long because of the heart condition and I could see valuable time ebbing away. On the other hand, I could feel the excitement once again as I got closer and closer to returning.

I had been out for about 10 months before making my return off the bench in another away trip to Posh. I think you could call Peterborough one of my least favourite away grounds because, if anything, this went even worse than my previous visit.

We were already 1-0 down when I was introduced after fellow defender Jake Buxton was sent off. Problem was that during my time on the pitch we shipped two further goals and one was my fault. I tried to play a forward pass to get us behind their defence, but it was cut out and they scored on the break.

Nigel Clough slammed the dressing room door afterwards and laid into us big time. His message was that, if you are 1-0 down, you don't make things worse by making needless mistakes. A 3-0 defeat was far worse than it need have been and could be costly as it damaged our goal difference. I won't repeat exactly what he called me, but he hadn't forgotten where I came from and he wasn't too impressed with what I'd just done. "I brought you on to kick and head the ball, not to play," he said. I sat slumped in my chair, taking his comments on the chin and generally feeling sorry for myself.

The other lads did much to ease my pain and allow me to understand the manager. They said to take his criticism as a compliment because he obviously thought I was worth talking to and could do better. It's when the manager ignores you, you know you're in the shit, they added.

I had the excitement of seeing the other side of the East Midlands derby when starting in another clash against Forest, this time at Pride Park. And I can tell you the atmosphere is every bit as intense when Derby are the hosts.

Again, it was a lunchtime kick off and we went into the game in confident mood after three successive victories over our rivals, starting with the ten-men triumph. By now Alex McLeish was Forest manager in the middle of a very short spell in charge as their new Kuwaiti owners rang the changes. We felt we had the better of the first half before Chris Cohen, now back from injury, got some revenge by slotting Forest ahead at the second attempt.

Nigel didn't panic at the break, challenging us to continue playing the same way and get back into the game. That happened very quickly when Conor Sammon dispossessed Simon Gillett and made an outstanding run before playing in that man Wardy who again finished in style. I never scored a goal for Derby and had one of my best chances during that second half. A corner found me unmarked ten yards out, but my header went over the bar.

It still surprises and thrills me how popular I am at Derby despite not playing that many games, but I would have been remembered even more fondly had I scored the winner against Forest. Instead, the match finished 1-1.

About two or three months after my return, I was struggling with another problem with the same knee. This time it was swelling badly and a scan revealed a microfracture. An operation was possible, but I was told that, given rest, I also had the option of playing on. This meant playing on a Saturday, then staying away from training Monday to Thursday.

I did this for about three to four months, and it suited me better than being sidelined again, but a couple of the more experienced players warned me to be careful that I didn't suffer any long-term damage.

My call up for the Republic's under 21 squad came whilst I was managing this knee condition. Nigel Clough was straight with me, pointing out his priority was that I played for Derby County and he didn't want this to be jeopardised through playing international football. He was happy to release me to join up with the Republic squad for the experience on condition that I told the manager I wasn't fit to play.

This could have been an awkward conversation, but the Republic's manager Noel King was very understanding. He thanked me for being upfront about my problem and allowed me to spend the week with my family in Dublin. This meant I was rested and buzzing when I returned to Derby in time for the trip to Sheffield Wednesday only for a problem to occur in the warmup.

Stepping up from light jogging to running, I felt my knee jarring. I told the physio that I didn't think I could sprint and he ordered me back inside to talk with Nigel Clough. The manager needed to submit the team sheet in five minutes, so it was up to me whether my name was on it. I gave it another go, but the knee jarred as soon as I tried to run. Cloughie wanted me to play and gave me a death stare, but I had no choice. Again, the manager's disappointment was a compliment. He was very keen for me to play and, in turn, I would have done anything to avoid letting him down.

However, it was time once again to face facts. I needed a second knee operation and this was going to be even more mentally tough. I was out of the game for another 11 months.

My recovery involved being tied to the CPM machine, labelled by Shaun Barker as the 'machine of death' – and he knew from bitter experience. I literally had to stay on that machine eight hours a day, bending and straightening my knee. That effectively put my life on hold. For the first time in my life, I genuinely considered if all this was worthwhile. I'd gone through a serious heart scare and a long-term knee injury, now I was at a very low ebb. But, no, I couldn't allow myself to think that way. Again, I used my heart experience as a guide. I'd beaten that, so why not this?

I didn't speak with too many people about my problems because the last thing I wanted was a sympathy vote. I wanted to be treated on equal terms as any other footballer. In the end it was a 10 or 11 month haul before I was back jogging with the first team lads and got a great reception from Nigel Clough and the rest of the staff.

Nigel still backed me, saying he was looking forward to seeing me play again, but fate took a different course. We had started the season indifferently and desperately needed a positive result in the first East Midlands derby at the City Ground. Although it was too early for me to be back in the squad, I was with the team that unfortunate Saturday lunchtime.

Nigel realised how much was on the line. Victory on Trentside would almost certainly have bought him more time. To make things even more intense, former Derby manager Billy Davies was back in the Forest dugout for a second time, having been given a big cheque book by the club's Kuwaiti owners to finance an expected promotion push.

For some reason, there's a big crossover of managers across the A52 with Brian Clough himself, McClaren and Davies among those to have held the top job at both clubs. And there's also a history of managers getting the sack after a derby defeat. It turned out to be a typical dour and fierce affair with Forest grabbing a first half lead when defender Jack Hobbs scored with a header from a corner.

There was nothing much between the sides for the rest of the game, although we needed a late penalty save from Lee Grant to deny Darius Henderson a second goal from the penalty spot. Margins in football are often very thin. This was Forest's first victory in five games and our first defeat away from Pride Park, yet Davies soaked up the adulation of their fans and the decision was made to sack Nigel Clough.

We were back home in our apartments when the dramatic news came through. The players all got messages on our mobile phones that the manager had gone before I switched on the TV for confirmation. It was an emotional moment for me, and I wasn't the only one. Nigel brought us together both on and off the pitch. It didn't matter whether you were 33 years old or 18; if he liked you and you were prepared to buy into what he wanted and work very hard, he would treat you like one of his own.

Football-wise his tactics were straightforward. He wanted defenders to do the basics, such as head and clear the ball, midfielders to play from box to box and be creative, wide players to get the ball into the opposition's penalty area and strikers to score goals. Not having much money for new players probably drew us closer as a squad. We weren't the best team in the

Championship, but Nigel stabilised the club and we were never a million miles from making a genuine promotion challenge.

My judgement may have been coloured by the brilliant way Nigel Clough treated me throughout my rollercoaster Derby career, but I don't think his contribution to the club was ever fully recognised. He took the job with The Rams at a very low ebb and, after winning an initial battle against the drop, kept us in mid-table despite working on a very restricted budget. Despite constantly having to reduce the wage bill and not bringing in many new signings, Nigel moulded together a squad, including young players whom he helped bring through, and made us into a family. The spirit around Pride Park was always good as he got on with everybody.

Nigel was the perfect choice for Derby as he knew the club, knew the area and was a working class man with his feet firmly on the ground. I think Derby fans now may look at subsequent managers and wonder what Nigel could have achieved.

However, because of Derby County's great history, consolidation at the second level of English football wasn't considered success. With the benefit of hindsight and considering the club's current predicament, fans probably still wonder what might have happened had Nigel Clough either been given more financial backing or time.

Looking at my time off the pitch, Derby became more and more my second home. When I was 17, l moved into more digs outside the city centre with Jeff Hendrick and Graham Kelly and again stayed there for about a year. This place was run by Rosie Bushell, a lovely woman who I still stay in touch with today. All this helped me with growing up whilst the Derby first team lads ensured we felt at home when we joined up with them.

The group consisted of lads between the ages of 18 and 32 and we all got on extremely well. There was no sense that the more experienced players tested us out before accepting us. They were always prepared to help and encourage us, whilst also putting us in our place when necessary.

From the age of 18, I moved into an apartment in the centre of Derby, living on my own for the first time in my life. This was also a breakthrough as I began to realise how good this could be. Mum came over every now and then from Ireland and I also had friends staying. Finally, I made the move into a house with

Jeff and Conor Doyle, another of the first team who now plays his soccer in America. Some fellow first teams used to come over for darts tournaments and a few drinks and, likewise, we were welcome at their places. He won't like me saying it but in the Anglo Scottish battles with midfielder Paul Coutts I reckon I won about nine times out of ten!

We became a very close-knit group and this was helped by Nigel Clough taking us to Spain, New York and Miami for trips. Everybody got to know each other, and this was one reason we had each other's backs on the pitch. Perhaps it was helped by not too many new signings coming into the side. Instead, we grew together as people and footballers and the boss was particularly good at bringing in academy lads such as Mason Bennett, Will Hughes and Callum Ball.

You can never underestimate how important it is to have a united dressing room. You realise it when you experience one that isn't. Off the pitch during our time under Nigel Clough, I developed friendships with several members of the squad and we were a close group.

I lived in two different places with fellow Irishman Jeff Hendrick, moving from our first house in slightly comical circumstances. We'd both been away for the weekend with the squad before arriving back home on the Sunday evening. The following morning, I asked Jeff if he'd left the window open and he said no. I didn't think anything more of it but when we returned after training both of us discovered that a lot of our electrical equipment, including a laptop and a PlayStation, had been stolen. Talk about dozy footballers!

Seriously, though, the break-in at our house changed things for Jeff and me. We couldn't so easily view it as our home after that. So, a couple of months or so later we moved into an apartment in Duffield. This was a place where we felt more relaxed, each having a sofa recliner to ourselves to chill out in the evenings. We lost none of our team feeling as Johnny Russell lived in the next block and was one of our regular visitors. Another was James Bailey, or Bales, as we called him. He was Manchester-based but we put up a blow-up mattress and he stayed with us when it was more convenient.

Bales knew how to bring the worst out of me diet wise. For

whilst Jeff stuck more to healthy food, I was always up for being nudged in the other direction. Quite often, Bales suggested a Chinese – Jeff would say 'no thanks' and I'd cave in, usually at the second time of asking.

I'm making no apologies for this or the fact that we went out socialising like other young people of a similar age. We were essentially two 19 or 20-year-olds living away from home, enjoying ourselves and not doing any harm. Instead, I think it's quite important to remember that footballers are human beings – and mostly young ones at that.

All young people live and learn, often through their mistakes, and we were no different. We knew how far we could go socially. We never went out on the night before a game but could socialise on a Saturday night. Nigel Clough was good with us. His view was that we should go out as a team and create more joint memories. He didn't come with us but trusted us to behave sensibly.

This was where that Derby squad was unusual. There were no cliques and the players from different age groups all got on together. The older ones would be there to give us a slap on the wrist if anyone crossed the line. In addition, Jeff and I would sometimes go out on a Wednesday and Thursday night for a few drinks. And it wasn't unusual for us to go down the pub on a Sunday to watch a Premier League game on Sky Sports.

There was a short time when we were both out injured. That was an opportunity to have a look at how busy the town was – and it was! This type of thing is harder for young players today as the social media age has grown and you are more and more likely to be captured on someone's camera phone.

Things were a bit different when Steve McClaren took over. He had worked as a coach under Sir Alex Ferguson at Manchester United where they were less lenient. He came with different ideas which included more emphasis on our lifestyle off the pitch.

Under Nigel Clough I matured as a person whilst McClaren developed me in ways that I wasn't expecting as a footballer Under Nigel, I was expected to kick it and head it and generally perform the old-fashioned role as a defender. Yes, I could pass a football but that was secondary to doing the basics well. I was expected to immerse myself in learning the craft of a defender and that was how I was brought up.

McClaren brought in a more possession-style of football that saw Derby County play some of the best stuff they have produced in recent years. And this inevitably meant the goalkeeper and defenders played out from the back rather than hit the ball long for the forwards to chase. I didn't see myself as this kind of player and this was probably one reason why the likes of Jake Buxton, Richard Keogh and Zak Whitbread were ahead of me in the pecking order.

McClaren looked for players who fitted his style but was also able to improve lads through his coaching. He had a reputation before he came to Derby as one of the best coaches in the business, leading to his ill-fated time in charge of the England national team, and he lived up to those standards at Pride Park. Buxton was one of the lads who blossomed under McClaren's guidance, looking an almost completely different player. On the other hand, McClaren had players such as Craig Bryson, Patrick Bamford, Jeff Hendrick, George Thorne, Will Hughes and Andre Wisdom who already complemented his style very well.

I think this is the key as to whether playing out from the back works. When he went to the other end of the A52 to manage Nottingham Forest, he probably didn't have the players to play his way and he ended up being dismissed in double quick time. I don't regard either Nigel's 'roll your sleeves up and be a solid team approach' or McClaren's slick passing football as being definitively right or wrong. They both have their place depending on personnel and circumstances and both worked well at Derby County during my time there.

Although I wasn't in the first team under McClaren, it was a great time to be around the club. In training I was learning more and more, particularly about how to handle the ball and play out from the back. The team flourished and, whilst I was disappointed not to play, we all felt that we were going places.

Richard Keogh and Jake Buxton were unstoppable at the back and there was a buzz and confidence about Derby County that convinced us that we were heading for the Premier League. Irony of ironies, we totally turned the tables on Forest with an unbelievable performance at Pride Park that has also gone into local folklore.

After looking a good bet for the top six, Forest were on the slide and the pressure was on Billy Davies to get his promotion push back on track. In contrast, we were still in the hunt for automatic promotion, despite not having scored for four games. Everything clicked for us after Craig Bryson ended our goal drought with a deflected shot in the sixth minute. It was 3-0 and almost game over by half time and our domination continued afterwards with Bryson completing his hat trick from the penalty spot. An incredible 5-0 scoreline equalled Derby's biggest ever win over Forest and was enough for their owners to pull the plug on Billy Davies.

The football gods, however, are anything but predictable and we slipped into the play off places in the last few weeks. Nevertheless, everything seemed to be in our favour at Wembley in the play-off final against QPR. We dominated the match well before Rangers were reduced to ten men, yet the tension increased with every minute that we were unable to find that elusive opening goal.

The tie went into extra time before the seemingly inevitable happened – one break, one shot, one goal and our bubble was burst by Bobby Zamora.

I still had a year left on my deal when I got a phone call that summer from Motherwell manager Steve McCall, wanting to take me to Scotland on a six-month loan. I wanted Steve McClaren to say I was going nowhere. Instead, he recommended the move, saying it would put me in the shop window and set me up for a new adventure. After all I had been through at Derby, maybe it was time to move elsewhere and create more memories.

I didn't agree with McClaren but, looking back, I understand his point. In fact, I'm grateful to him. Had I stayed at Derby, I could have wasted another year without playing first team football. Had he avoided or fudged the issue, I would probably have seen out the last year of my three-year contract at Derby and missed out on playing first team football.

Leaving Derby was nevertheless a big wrench. This was the first place that I had lived since leaving home and I was there for five or six years. I played football at a high level with a club I loved, made friends and Derby became my comfort zone, my second home.

CHAPTER THREE
SCOTTISH ROLLERCOASTER AND BUSINESS WITH NATHAN JONES

MOTHERWELL had finished second in the Scottish Premier League the previous season and just taken part in a Europa League tie, so it looked like a good move for me. In addition, Stuart McCall had managed my brother James when he was at Bradford City, so I knew something about him.

I thought a loan move might be a way of playing myself back into contention at Derby, but McClaren put me right, saying that my career at Pride Park had reached a stalemate, after successive highs and lows, and that I needed to go out into the bigger world of football. I was nervous about going to Motherwell. It was similar in a way to starting from square one at a new school.

I was looking forward to finding out what the Scottish Premier League was all about and Stuart McCall and his assistant Kenny Black were brilliant when they spoke with me. Centre back Steve McManus was one of the first to welcome me into the fold and I was also playing alongside club legend Stephen Hamill, skipper and central midfielder Keith Lesley and Ian Vigurs, another whom I got on very well with. I also formed a central defensive partnership with Geordie Simon Ramsden.

I was pleased to play the full 90 minutes in our opening game against St Johnstone and again at Ross County where we recorded our first win. Our full-on start also included a local derby against Hamilton in the League Cup when we went out on penalties and then the ultimate test at Celtic. This was a particularly poignant day for me because I grew up as a Celtic fan and always imagined what it would be like to go to Celtic

Park one day. Now it was happening and I was playing rather than spectating!

Whilst the home fans were blasting out Irish Rover among their old Irish songs, I was on the pitch secretly smiling and singing along.

We were playing against a formidable Celtic side, including the great Virgil Van Dijk at centre back, John Guidetti and my former Derby teammate Kris Commons further forward. Unsurprisingly, our backs were against the wall for much of the afternoon, but we got our noses in front and had a very good chance to make it 2-0. We ended up getting an excellent point from a 1-1 draw. I felt that I'd played well and got off to a good start with my new club.

I found the Scottish Premier League to be a mixture of everything. From an English point of view, the sides varied from Championship to League One or League Two standard. One week you would be playing Celtic, Rangers, Aberdeen or Dundee United who were of a higher standard and played good football, next you'd pitch up against Partick Thistle or Inverness and had to be ready for a more physical battle. This meant the difference between needing to be at the top of my game to deal with high quality opponents to having the shit kicked out of me! Altogether a very interesting experience!

As far as the fan base was concerned, it was very different from Derby. Whereas I'd played in front of 30,000 crowds, the home attendance at Motherwell was more like 3,000 to 4,000. This, too, was an eyeopener for me. The supporters got behind us and backed the team, but the buzz of a big crowd was replaced by sometimes being able to hear individual shouts and complaints of fans.

McCall was a very good man manager who made you want to play for him. Unfortunately, he suffered because of how expectations had risen from the previous season. With results now not going our way, it led to the manager leaving the club which was a tough situation for me.

I was gutted because I enjoyed playing under McCall and he had wanted me at the club. In contrast, I knew very little about his successor Ian Baraclough, except that he had played with my cousin at Scunthorpe United. Certainly, I didn't know about him as a manager.

I hoped that, as a former centre back, he would be good for me but also realised that he would have his own ideas. Certain players didn't match up to those and I was one of them. Nevertheless, I threw myself into training and signed a six-month extension. The new manager said that I wasn't one of the most imposing centre backs physically. My reply was that I didn't get beaten too often in the air, nor did forwards get past me.

Baraclough restored me to the starting line-up after presumably changing his opinion. I started a few games and had a couple of chats with the new boss who was worried about the number of yellow cards that I was picking up.

I admit that I was picking up more cautions than I had at Derby. This was partly my fault and partly the way the game was officiated in the SPL. Some were soft as strikers went down when barely touched. Officials seemed to give strikers the benefit of the doubt which didn't help me. Yet I cringed at some of my tackles which could have resulted in me seeing red. My defence was that I was still learning the game at 21 years of age, having had a limited number of first team opportunities at Derby. None of this lessoned my enjoyment at Motherwell. Here I was playing first team football in a good league.

Baraclough then left me out for a couple of weeks which was disappointing. The manager had brought in three or four new signings from England but there was no immediate upturn in results.

I decided to ask Baraclough why I wasn't in the side. The first thing he said was that the yellow cards were a slight issue, followed by a comment that he wanted more 'presence' from his centre backs.

That confused me. Was I losing headers? Was I losing tackles? Or being beaten for pace? Again, the manager agreed I wasn't. In that case, I couldn't understand what he meant by lacking presence. I'm a reasonable height at 6'1" but he preferred his centre backs a couple of inches taller as highlighted by the signing of Louis Lang, who had played for him at Notts County. I hadn't done amazingly well back in the first team during the last months of the season but well enough, in my view, to believe that I'd be kept on.

A stomach bug kept me out of the crucial last couple of weeks of the season and the crunch play off against Rangers. In fact, I was struggling so much that I wasn't well enough to even travel to watch our superb 3-1 win at Ibrox in the first leg. I loved watching the return game as we convincingly beat one of Scotland's super clubs 3-0 at home.

Yet the euphoria of celebrating victory and survival in the Scottish Premier League with teammates and supporters was tinged with mixed feelings for me because of what happened afterwards.

It had been a mixed season for the club and for me personally. I'd seen it as an exciting new start after becoming out of favour at Derby, instead Motherwell had been fighting for their lives and I was in and out of the team. The way that it ended was a perfect example of that rollercoaster – there we were rescuing our season, yet the best I could do was watch from the stands. Then just two or three days later even that good feeling was snatched away.

Ian Baraclough invited all the players in one by one to discuss his plans for the following season. And it soon became clear that I wasn't in them. The reasons he gave me were excuses – best he could think of rather than speak the harsh truth as McClaren had done.

He wanted to slim down his first team squad to 18 or 19 players and they all needed to be able to train on all surfaces including astroturf. Baraclough knew full well that counted me out as, because of the knee injuries that I suffered at Derby County, I couldn't train on astroturf. But was that sufficient reason to show me the door? Had he wanted me at Motherwell, I'm sure it would have been a minor issue.

So, instead of having a break and preparing for another exciting year in Scotland, I flew back to Dublin without a club. That was far more worrying for me than the average fan would think. For a couple of months, I had to find the self-motivation to go to the gym daily and keep myself fit whilst the phone wasn't ringing. Ok, I'd played a reasonable number of games for two big clubs in Derby and Motherwell, but I wasn't established enough to know for certain that another club wanted me. It was like those very difficult days at Derby when I began my rehabilitation not knowing if I'd ever make it back onto a football field. Now

I didn't even have the security of having a club, a contract and money coming in.

I was still in Dublin on July 2, roughly a month before the start of the new season when that all changed. My agent phoned with some positive news – Luton Town wanted to take me on trial!

Today The Hatters have just become a Premier League side after triumphing at Wembley against Coventry City in the Championship play off final – that's an unbelievable achievement considering that they were a Conference side not so long ago and where they were when I joined them. Much of the credit for their amazing rise must go to Nathan Jones who has had two very successful spells at Kenilworth Road. Yet my experience was very different.

I'm not influenced either by the fact that Jones has twice failed in recent years at supposedly bigger and better clubs, Stoke City and Southampton. Instead, I'm just explaining my own Luton Town story – a year and a few months that began with high expectations and a lot of enjoyment and ended with me at rock bottom. My heart condition at Derby didn't finish me, but I was so disillusioned at Kenilworth Road that I so nearly packed my bags and went home to Dublin.

The timing of my initial joining was tight. They were due to fly out to Portugal in a couple of days for 10 days of pre-season training. Could I make it? You bet, I could. I immediately decided to fly to Luton to meet manager John Still before going out to Portugal.

Still had steered Luton back into the EFL after a frustratingly long spell in the Conference. But before I could even think about playing a part in the Hatters' overdue revival, I had to do enough to win myself a deal. I went out to Portugal with no guarantees. I was a free agent and there were no obligations either way. But it was made clear that, providing the 10 days went well, there could be a contract waiting for me.

Here I was on a plane with a bunch of strangers. Joining up with a new club is never easy but this was even more so. Usually there'd be at least one player in the squad that a new recruit knows or has some connection with. I knew literally nothing about any of them.

To increase my sense of isolation, I was put in a hotel room on my own because Paddy McCourt, a lad who I later became particularly good friends with, was given a couple of days extra off after his international commitments with Northern Ireland.

Pre-season being what it is, our schedule was gruelling. We were all given bikes to cycle to and from training – and then again for a second session. There was one friendly against Farense in the Algarve which we won with me even scoring a header.

I knew that had gone well, but the real icebreaker with my new teammates didn't see me emerge with much credit. In fact, I couldn't remember too much about it!

After all the hard work, we were allowed a night out as a group. The lads went to Albufeira for a typical footballers' drinking session. Those meant drinks, drinks and more drinks. We went from venue to venue, including an Irish Guinness bar, before I found myself sat outside a kebab shop with one of the players at around 1am. We'd become detached from the rest of the group, having no idea where they were.

All I can remember is that I was really, really pissed. Next a hen party walked by sporting 'shots. Did we want some? If the question included drink the answer was 'yes'. It tasted like pure vodka, was very strong and totally wiped me out. I was out on my feet and sick in the street. Worse still, I had no way of contacting any of the other lads and needed somehow to make my own way back to the hotel.

I climbed into a taxi, not having much idea how long the journey was. All I had was my hotel key, so at least I could tell the driver where to go. When we finally got there, I was 150 Euros lighter. Ouch! I hadn't expected that. I was sick again on the steps leading up to the hotel but that's about all I can remember. I found my room and slept it off as best I could, getting up at between 10am and 11am next morning.

How did I get home? I was beginning to feel very anxious, knowing that I'd made a massive show of myself. Meeting up with the rest of the lads, there were cries of 'look who is here' and 'he's alive!' At first, I felt embarrassed but then I realised what was happening. This was my initiation at Luton Town. By making a fool of myself, I'd become one of the lads and instantly broken down most of the social barriers.

Back in England, the news was good. The manager was impressed with how I'd performed on the training ground and in the friendly – and hadn't seen me on the night out! He offered me a two-year contract. "Brilliant," I replied. I signed without a second's thought.

Everything looked good. After consolidating back in League Two, Still made nine or ten new signings with a view to pushing on. His side included Paddy McCourt, Craig Mackail-Smith, Jack Marriott, Dan Potts, Josh McQoid and Cameron McGeehan. I moved into an apartment with skipper and fellow centre back, Steve McNulty, who was brilliant with me. Perhaps it was the Scouse and Irish connection? He looked out for me and was there for me which was ideal as I set out on an adventure with a new club.

Perfect! I was enjoying my new life at Luton. My new teammates were great and we started to have a good laugh together as well as to enjoy our football. I played a couple of games and was in and out of the team as Still, with a big squad, seemed to field one team in League Two and another in the League Cup.

The manager sprung a surprise before our home tie against Bristol City. Still showed us the line up in training and there I was – in central midfield! I'd never thought of myself as anything other than a defender but wasn't overawed. The manager saw me in the role of the holding midfielder, basically a defender in front of the back four. I told him that I was confident I could do the job for him – and I did. We won 3-1 and I played well. I featured in the same position in the following league game against Portsmouth, but with Still making regular changes was then slotted back into defence.

Nevertheless, when a huge home League Cup tie against Premier League Stoke City loomed, I chatted with the skipper about the possibility of Still picking me again in midfield. And that's what he did. I had a big task. That Stoke side included Shay Given in goal, Phil Bardsley, Stephen Ireland, Marko Arnautovic and Peter Crouch, not to mention a former Barcelona star Bojan in the number ten role – and therefore the main man I had to stop.

I was detailed to keep a very close eye on him. Wherever he went, I was to follow. And I did. Unfortunately, there were a few complications with my teammates. For, as I tracked my man even when he picked the ball up from Given, our midfielders wanted me to close down gaps behind them. I can't have done too badly though as Bojan was taken off towards the end and we were performing creditably despite falling behind to a goal from Jonathan Walters. The roof nearly came off Kenilworth Road when Cameron McGeehan grabbed the equaliser in the 90th minute.

One all meant 30 minutes of extra time with our home crowd giving us raucous backing. We went close to nicking it, but no more goals meant a penalty shootout and, fortunately, I was low on the list. Having cramp in parts of my legs that I didn't even know existed after 120 gruelling minutes meant that I was quite happy to be 10th choice.

As the successful kicks went in, I was desperate for us to win and also a bit worried that I might be needed to take a spot kick after all. Finally, defender Scott Griffiths hit the bar with his penalty and we went out 8-7 after a great night of cup football.

That was as close as I got to having one of football's ultimate tests. I never did take a penalty and wasn't involved in many shootouts. The only spot kicks I took were way back in my youth with Cherry Orchard.

Things then started to go wrong for me after I had a poor game in a 4-3 home defeat at the hands of Carlisle United. It was a disastrous afternoon as we let a 3-1 lead slip in the final 25 minutes and I was one of three defenders on the floor when the visitors got their equaliser. Afterwards I found out how horrible social media can be. I'd suffered criticism before, but this became relentless. Basically, I was 'shit' and should 'leave our club'. The abuse went on and on. It didn't matter what I put out on Twitter; the message would be much the same.

And, yes, it hurt my confidence. Dad hit the nail on the head by warning that social media was a game of two halves – if I accepted praise, I'd also have to expect the opposite. Opinions were like arseholes, he said, everyone has one! If I couldn't handle that, I needed to remove myself from it. So, I deleted my Twitter account.

The real turning point for me at Luton was the sacking of John Still a week before Christmas when I wasn't in the team and things weren't going well on the pitch.

In came Nathan Jones for his first managerial post after being first team coach at Premier League Brighton. Although I suffered under Jones, I can understand why he was successful. He steadied the ship that season and then secured promotion from League Two and they were second in League One when he made his ill-fated move to Stoke City. Later he returned to Kenilworth Road and took The Hatters to the play off semi final in 2021-22 before the Saints job came along.

Coming from Brighton, Jones had the prestige to demand things were done his way at a lower club. His talent was as a very good coach and the players bought into his style of play. Nobody can take that away from him although Luton fans may have mixed feelings because he left them twice.

A new manager almost always brings a clean slate whereby players who might not have been in favour with the former boss feel that they have another chance. That happened for all John Still's players bar one. Me! Apart from occasionally being an unused substitute, I never featured at all under Nathan Jones. Not a single minute on the pitch.

At first, I didn't question him but, when I did, I never got a satisfactory answer. "Nothing against you, it's business," he told me repeatedly. But what kind of business? I surmised that maybe, because he wanted his side to play out from the back, he didn't fancy me. Had I been given a chance to play his way and made mistakes, I'd have held my hand up and said, 'fair enough'. But still it was silence. He barely spoke with me.

Come April and, with Luton's season drifting towards a safe finish, Jones pulled me into his office and pointed out the obvious that I hadn't been getting game time. Conference side Southport had asked to take me for a month and he thought it was a great idea. I would go there, hopefully play all seven games remaining and then be better equipped to challenge for a place at Luton Town.

I agreed. The one thing that I wanted more than any other was to play first team football again. There had been precious little of it at Luton, yet I went to Southport still considering myself a Hatters player. Dino Maamria was in charge of a Lancashire side in the middle of a relegation battle. I credit him for giving me a new lease of life and for that I'll always be grateful. I travelled up there on the Friday to meet the boss and went straight into the team for the following afternoon's home game against Halifax.

There I was with that 'first day at school' feeling again. I walked into the dressing room knowing nobody and with the rest of the team understandably a bit quiet before an important game. Maamria had a habit of addressing the side from number one to 11 before the game, making observations about what had gone before and what he hoped to see in the following 90 minutes. As he began his pre-match talk, the thought went through my mind 'what is he going to say about me?'

After talking about the other centre back, he introduced me as his new signing and said that he was very surprised to have got me in his team because I should be playing at a higher level. I was a no-nonsense defender in the air and on the deck and would help them a lot in their relegation fight. This gave me mixed feelings. On the positive side, it was the first time that I'd been praised for months. I'd got very little feedback from Nathan Jones and hadn't felt valued. To hear Maamria's opinion gave me a lift, particularly as he obviously knew a fair deal about me. On the other hand, it was slightly embarrassing. The way the manager had bigged me up, there was now added pressure to do well when I hadn't played professional football for months.

Although we lost 1-0, I played really well and started to feel part of the group. I went on to play in all seven games and helped Southport steer clear of the dreaded drop. As an added personal bonus, I scored the first goal of my professional career in a 3-3 draw against Welling United. Believe it or not, that match got me abuse from Luton fans for surrendering a 3-1 lead. It went on the lines of: "That's what happens when you've got Mark O'Brien in your side." Cheers!

Some Southport lads bought into me and gave me a lot of encouragement. Chief among them was veteran midfielder Gary Jones, who played more than 700 games and broke Rochdale's appearance record. He was brilliant, saying he didn't know what I was doing playing at this standard because I should be much higher. He knew that I'd been through a rough time but told me to keep doing what I was doing.

I was delighted. Those words helped me prove a point to myself. I needed to show that I was still a good player after my confidence had taken a battering at Luton. I even got a card from the whole team, thanking me for helping them. That was such a kind gesture. I felt as if I'd truly contributed something.

This meant that I returned to Luton after the loan with my confidence restored. After playing seven full games and doing well, I remembered the manager's promise that I'd put myself back into contention for a first team place.

First game back was a lengthy trip to Hartlepool on a Tuesday night. As usual, 19 of us travelled – the starting eleven, seven substitutes and one extra. In these circumstances, the 'spare' man doesn't normally find out until a few hours before kick off. You've guessed it, I was that man!

Nathan Jones said that I had just returned from my loan and he had decided to go instead with a defender who had been training with us while I'd been away. Something wasn't right here.

Next up was another long journey to Carlisle and, with one of the central defenders out injured, I was confident of at least being on the bench after again being named in the travelling party. But no. Instead, the manager put an 18-year-old on the bench and I again sat in the stand. I wasn't happy. After feeling optimistic about going back to Kenilworth Road, I'd been on two of the longest trips of the season and still not kicked a ball.

Again, the manager's explanation was sketchy. He said that it had been a long and difficult week, next week was a new one – he'd figure something out. So, I went back into training and saw out what I would kindly describe as an up and down season.

I was very happy to join Luton, a club with a proud history and now back on the up. I felt wanted by John Still even if I didn't get a regular place. Then things went downhill after Nathan Jones took over. I was embarrassed getting texts from friends and contacts asking me why I wasn't in the team. After what happened at Derby County, I was often asked if I was injured.

But, no, this wasn't Mark O'Brien, the injury prone defender. Instead, I didn't know much more than they did. Nathan Jones had said very little, apart from repeating that old line of 'it's business'.

When we returned for pre-season training, Jones took me into his office for a chat. Still no encouragement. Instead, he was taking my squad number off me – again a matter of 'business'. Luton and I were moving in different directions – Nathan Jones didn't want me with the team at all.

I was being treated like I was being disciplined. I'd done nothing to fall out with Jones or anyone else and the manager acknowledged that I wasn't a bad lad and it was nothing personal. Yet I was being ordered to train with teenagers from the academy.

Talk about being an outcast! The first team flew off for a training camp in Austria without me. The academy lads jetted off to Italy and, being the outsider at the grand old age of 24, I wasn't with them either. So, I spent the next three important weeks of pre-season almost totally by myself. I trained as usual, lifted weights, went on the treadmill, did all the fitness work that I could, showered and went home.

Welcome to the harsh world of football that most fans don't think about. Most presume footballers have an amazing life – money, acclaim, playing the game they love. Instead, I was living on my own many miles from home after Steve McNulty moved to Tranmere, training on my own and had no prospect of playing football.

I was becoming very lonely, with no friends to call on locally aside from my teammates and feeling in no man's land. I had no security nor an idea of where I was heading. All I could do was keep my head down, do my job and get through this.

In these circumstances, everyone needs a friendly face, someone with your best interests at heart and at Luton that man was Andy Awford, one of the academy coaches. He saw my predicament and did his best to help, putting on fitness sessions to keep me ticking over. But there was no chance of getting myself match fit without proper training and playing games.

I didn't have an agent as I'd decided I was big enough to talk for myself. But I got in touch with my friend Mark O'Brien – my namesake who'd helped me in my move to Derby. And he put me in touch with Tranmere Rovers manager, Gary Brabin, who was looking to add another defender to his Conference squad.

By coincidence, Tranmere were travelling to Dublin in a week's time for a five-day stay. The hotel rooms had already been booked but were within 30 minutes of my family home. Was this the bit of luck I needed?

That gave my sessions with Andy extra impetus. "Remember, you're doing this for Tranmere," he said. I had my spell training with them, plus the added bonus of being able to spend some time with my family before returning to Luton, by which time the first team and the academy were back from their respective trips.

I felt like a spare part training with teenagers, but I always did my best. I went into work, shook hands and said 'good morning' to the manager and got on with the training. I did my best to pass on any useful advice to the youngsters and was available whenever someone dropped out of the first team training group to take their place.

I was calling on every ounce of resilience that I'd gleaned from everything that had happened. If I could battle back from open heart surgery, two very bad knee injuries and being rejected by Motherwell, I could handle this. I wasn't going to allow Nathan Jones or anyone else to break me.

That said, my love for football was fading quickly. If this was 'business', I couldn't stick too much more of it. The temptation to pack my bags and head off home to Dublin was certainly there.

It's one thing not playing, it's another being left totally in limbo. I was having a horrible time and getting myself into a bad head space. The only game I played was a friendly between the under 18s and under 16s and I was captain of the under 18s. I recall Andy's words: "Be an example for the young players. Don't do yourself a disservice. Go out and perform for you." I played about 60 minutes. It was very frustrating, watching teenagers making mistakes. It was like banging my head against a wall.

The manager hadn't spoken with me at all during pre-season when an open day training session was held at Kenilworth Road. This is an event when fans get a close-up view of the players going about their work. The problem was nobody bothered to tell me. So, I turned up at an empty training ground where I phoned Nathan Jones and he told me to come to the stadium. I put in a hard shift and won some praise from Mick Harford, who was working under Nathan Jones and was, of course, a Luton legend (he even claimed to once score an own goal to help keep them up!).

Nevertheless, next day I was back training with the academy. What was going on? I tried extra hard to train better than the young lads, keep my standards up and not burn any bridges. Then came Deadline Day, that day of madness which the media loves because it provides them with a host of stories but often a very difficult time for footballers.

I wasn't expecting anything although, if a club came in for me, I would have been interested. All I wanted was a contract and the chance to play football. The financial side was purely about giving me security, knowing that I could pay my bills.

What followed was almost a pantomime My phone rang first at noon. It was Nathan Jones. After saying nothing more than 'good morning' for months, he asked about my welfare. A few pleasantries later came the punchline. "OB, there's a year left on your contract and we're looking to pay you up. Then you can leave Luton Town and find another club as a free agent. We have a solicitor here until 5pm – let me know your answer."

This came as a shock. Nathan Jones had five weeks of pre-season to suggest how we could both move forward. But there had been nothing. Now, at the last moment, he had put me on the spot.

I said that I didn't know what to do and we left it at that – he was going to ring back later. I phoned my cousin and professional footballer, Clifford Byrne, the closest person that I had to an agent. I told him about Luton's offer and that I couldn't guarantee getting another. He advised me to say no.

I used my contacts, including Mark O'Brien and Southport and Tranmere, the two clubs who had shown an interest, to try to fix myself up. Tranmere were interested but on condition that they were able to offload another defender.

Again, Clifford opened my eyes. "Don't accept anything unless you've got another club. The moment you sign that paper, you are out of Luton Town Football Club and you're on your own. Nathan Jones is trying to put pressure on you – and the deadline's 11pm, not 5pm."

It was 5pm. My phone rang. "What's going on, OB?" asked the manager. "I can't accept it," I replied. "I don't have anywhere to go. I have an apartment to pay for and nowhere else to live."

The manager's tone changed. He was starting to have a go at me, saying that I wasn't backing myself to get fixed up. I explained it wasn't about money but looking out for my future. I had zero security if I signed away my contract. Suddenly the solicitor was going to be there until 8pm for a final answer. Clifford's advice remained the same. "Luton Town must look after you if you are their player. The moment you sign that piece of paper, they don't have to do anything."

Ok, the pay-out would be useful short term, but for how long? If I went to another club on trial as a free agent and got injured, I'd be liable for my medical costs. Also, I wouldn't be able to afford to rent the apartment for long without money coming in.

Nathan Jones rang again at 8pm. What was my decision? I knew Tranmere were having problems with their side of the possible deal, so I had nowhere to go. I wanted to stay at Luton Town but was unhappy at not being given an opportunity in months. "So, you are blaming me then?" said Jones, becoming more defensive. "You blame me as a scapegoat for the fact that you can't get a game."

Then he used what he thought was a threat. "If you don't accept this, I'll bring you into training seven days a week. "You'd be doing me a favour, boss, because that would make me fitter," I replied.

Jones said he'd ring back in an hour. "He's giving you an ultimatum," said Clifford. "He's probably trying to bring in another player and he can't do so unless he clears your wages. Ask yourself this: would you rather wake up tomorrow morning with a pay-off but without a club or still have a contract?"

That was my light bulb moment. I wasn't selfish or greedy. I had no security, and it was better for me to remain a Luton Town player. Of course, another club who wanted me to play would have been preferable but that wasn't on the table.

His final phone call arrived at 9.30pm. Nathan Jones wasn't pleased that I stood my ground. "This is not going to be easy for you," he said. "You are going to mess with your career. You've not played for four or five months and it will be another six until the next transfer window. See you Thursday." He hung up the phone. He was going to do everything possible to make my life a misery at Luton Town, again almost treating me in a disciplinary fashion.

But the night wasn't quite all over. At 10.30pm Luton

chairman Gary Sweet rang. He had always been fine with me but asked what was going on as the manager was going mad. "Gary, you know me, I'm not greedy. All I want is to play games, but I have no security and, if I can't find another club, I'll be forced to go home to Dublin." Gary was fine and promised that the club would get me out on loan. The transfer window only applied to the EFL, so there was still a chance of finding a Conference club.

Back in training, Nathan Jones claimed that I'd made the wrong decision because I didn't 'fancy my chances'. He could have got me fixed up at Yeovil, he added. So why didn't he when he knew I wanted to play?

Gary Sweet kept his word and I went back to Southport on loan only for my bad luck to strike again. Just a couple of weeks into the loan, I suffered a tear of fibres in and around my knee, quite a rare injury, in training and had to return to Luton.

In a strange way, though, what happened justified my decision to remain at Kenilworth Road. I'd given up my apartment in Luton as I was due to spend three months with Southport and then hopefully get fixed up permanently in the next transfer window. Instead, I was forced to return to the club for treatment, which I would have had to pay for if I hadn't got a contract, and needed affordable accommodation.

Best I could do was The Leaside Hotel which I paid for out of my own pocket because the club wouldn't fund it. Like an air bed and breakfast, this was a great place with staff being brilliant with me. They could see that I was down on my luck, highlighted by the amount of time I spent sleeping! I was existing rather than living and mindful that I needed to move on sooner rather than later.

I'd also like to thank Luton physio Simon Parselle, kit man Darren Cook and some of my teammates. Fellow Irishman Alan Sheehan, by then Luton's captain, was fantastic as he offered me a place to stay with him and his girlfriend. I will also always remember Paddy McCourt who had invited me into his family home the previous Christmas.

An Irish winger, Paddy was one of the most talented players that I played with. I knew Paddy from his Celtic days and there was a touch of Lionel Messi about him. Can't say better than that! Paddy has had his own ups and downs, but I got the chance to be close to him during my stay at Luton.

These kind people and Andy Awford helped to make my Luton journey more enjoyable. We all live and learn and I'm grateful in some ways for all of my experiences. But my time at Luton was a long way from the home that I found at Derby County – and now in Wales.

CHAPTER FOUR
WITH MR MOTIVATOR
GRAHAM WESTLEY

I WOULD like to put on record here that I owe a great deal to former Newport County manager, Graham Westley.

He was very different from any other boss that I had played for and I've highlighted just some of my experiences in this chapter. But, although his methods surprised me at times, I will never forget that when I most needed a break, he was the guy who believed in me enough to give me that chance. Save for him, I may well have packed my bags and flown back to Dublin for good after the end of my nightmare at Luton Town.

This part of my life started when I was enjoying Christmas at Clifford Byrne's home in Scunthorpe. He was kind enough to invite me to spend the festivities with him and his family which gave us the chance to talk through what was happening. He encouraged me to use my contacts and I sent a text to Dino Maamria, my recent manager at Southport, who had become Graham Westley's assistant at Newport County.

I asked him about joining Newport and he wanted to know if I was fit, mindful no doubt that I'd cut my second loan spell at Southport short and hadn't played since. On the positive side, he knew what I was capable of from my first loan spell when I'd shown that I could play at a higher level.

I told Dino honestly that I was in good physical condition and injury-free, but lacking match fitness because of not getting a game at Kenilworth Road. Above all, I needed minutes on the pitch.

Dino said to leave it with him and he would speak with Graham Westley. I didn't have to wait long for an answer. A few days later, after the New Year's Day match at Wycombe, Dino texted to say that the manager wanted to meet me.

I was back in Luton staying for a few days with my friend Alan Sheehan when Graham Westley invited me to a hotel in London. Although Alan didn't play for Westley, word gets round in football, and he gave me useful advice. He said that when Westley asked about my ambitions in football, I shouldn't sell myself short. Rather than say I wanted to be the best player in League Two, I should talk about being the best player in the world! A bit fanciful, maybe, but Westley was known for wanting players with ambition and self-belief.

Not only did I not feel like the best thing on the planet, I wasn't very confident about myself at all. My terrible time at Luton had eaten away at my self-confidence. Also, after being out of action for so long, there were nagging doubts about getting back to my best on the pitch.

I couldn't allow Westley to see these self-doubts. This was a rare chance to sell myself. We met in late afternoon and Westley marched into the hotel dressed from head to toe in his Newport gear. He looked me up and down and we had a coffee and a tea respectively whilst he tried to find out more about me. His knowledge of me was minimal, nothing more than what his assistant had told him. Luckily, he fully trusted Dino's opinion.

Asked what kind of player I was, I said that I was a typical no-nonsense, old-school defender who loved to kick it and head it. I said I was raring to show what I could do when inside I was feeling very low. I couldn't afford to blow this.

Westley told me about his managerial career starting with Stevenage, one of the clubs where he made his name. I will never forget his words. He said he was a 'Jose Mourinho/Sir Alex Ferguson' type of manager. Wow, that was something to live up to!

He said that he pushed his players to their physical limits and promised to let me know what he thought about me. Providing I worked very hard and came up to the mark, everything would be fine; if I fell short, however, he'd be first to tell me.

He was very up front about the 'terrible' situation the club was in. Newport were rock bottom of League Two several points from safety and he needed to change things very quickly. He was looking to bring in eight or nine players, including me. He was keen for me to make my debut at his old club Stevenage on the Saturday and I was happy to do just that.

But, first, we needed to sort out my situation at Luton Town. I was six months from the end of my contract and they knew nothing about my meeting with Graham Westley. I suggested returning to Luton and telling them first thing in the morning that I wanted to be released and paid up. That wasn't enough for Westley. That would take too long when he wanted me in the team at the weekend. So, he rang Gary Sweet there and then whilst I listened in.

Typically, he got straight to the point. He said I was with him and he wanted me to play for Newport on Saturday. Gary asked to speak with me and said again that I wouldn't kick another ball for Luton in my last six months. So, the club would pay me one month's wages and let me go.

One month? I wasn't happy. I was on £1100 a week at Luton and the club were prepared to pay up my contract in full when it suited them. Now the boot was partly on the other foot, they were playing hard ball. "Surely you can do better than that?" said Westley, who was listening. He suggested three months was fairer, but Gary wasn't for moving. He was indicating that Luton's finances were tight, but I knew the score.

Westley suggested a compromise. "We will take over Mark's contract for the six months, if you pay the month," he said. Then he hung up the phone. The two of us then carried on talking. Newport would guarantee paying me until the end of the season and then cover June and July if we stayed in the EFL.

His position was very clear – help his side to perform an unlikely salvage act and I'd be paid for the full six months and get a two-year contract afterwards. If, as was more likely, we dropped out of the league, my wages would finish at the end of the season and we would part ways.

What had Nathan Jones said about me not being confident enough to back myself? Now I was being asked to do so big time. After not having played football for months, I needed to believe in my own ability more than ever before.

The alternative was worse. Another six months on the sidelines and then try to find another club having not played for about a year. If I wasn't exactly confident now, how much more would I doubt myself then?

Nevertheless, this was a big decision and, ideally, I would have liked time. But there was none. Westley demanded a decision on the spot and I realised hesitation on my part could be regarded as a sign of weakness. So, I shook his hand and said that I was excited to be joining him at Newport County – excited, but very nervous.

What had I done? Nothing new – I left Dublin to play professional football and Graham Westley was offering me just that.

The money, although Luton were harsh on me, was secondary. I travelled back to Luton to get my stuff and say my goodbyes and thanks to Alan Sheehan for his support. Then I returned to Wales on the Thursday where they put me up in a hotel.

Reporting for training on the Friday, there was only one session between me and my big kick off 24 hours later. Yet again, I felt like a schoolboy on day one – didn't know any of my new teammates. Also, ironically, the session took place on astroturf.

What I didn't realise as we did defensive training drills was that all the other defenders felt much the same way. Westley had brought in a brand new back four. No pressure!

There are two ways such a situation can go. Either we would get an immediate lift from having new players onto the pitch or suffer because we weren't used to playing together. Day one turned out to be the latter. I played centre back as we conceded a couple of first half goals and, although the manager took consolation from our improvement after the interval, we eventually went down 3-1 – our eighth defeat on the spin that left us five points from safety.

This was my first fully professional game for nearly a year and was always going to be a physical challenge. Overall, I was proud of myself for how I played and getting through the full 90 minutes. I was tired towards the end and pretty sore afterwards but, considering the circumstances, I was pleased.

Westley's take was that his gamble was necessary because things had not been going well, but I'm sure there was a feeling of 'same old story' afterwards.

In the end I was one of seven new signings that the manager

made in the January transfer window. And we all soon found out that Graham Westley lived up to his words about working us to our limits. One of the players joked about whether I'd brought my spikes as we prepared for an early training session. He obviously knew how much running and gym work Westley liked to put us through.

I never enjoyed running – I hated it. Whether long distance or shorter track work, it wasn't my cup of tea. The only running I really enjoyed was on the pitch as part of my defensive duties. Nevertheless, I threw myself into training to honour my pledge to give 100 per cent effort towards the manager's bid to save us from relegation.

At one point, there were 25 lads standing in the gym each with five kilo weights in their right hand. We then did 50 repetitions with the weights in either hand before doing 25 press ups. The session ended with very tired arms holding the weights above our heads for a full five minutes.

This was clearly a test of physical strength and fitness plus mentality. Who would fail and let everyone else in the group down? Or would we look teammates in the eye and suffer for them?

Westley's philosophy was that, after running eight or ten kilometres in training, we would do the same when it really mattered on Saturday afternoon. No matter how talented you were, if you didn't put 100 per cent into training, you wouldn't be picked.

Overall, you could look at Westley's methods two ways. It made sense to train as you play rather than go through the motions. On the other hand, too much physical work in training can leave you leggy come kick off.

Westley was known for his unusual motivational methods which I got my first taste of on the Friday night before our next game against Colchester United. All the players received a text with a rousing message from Arnold Schwarzenegger, the famous actor and governor of California. Not something I was used to from any of my previous managers, but I was prepared to buy into it. Westley was always straight about wanting to get the absolute most from us, so it made sense to go along with his methods.

I got another 90 minutes under my belt as we finally ended

our long run of damaging defeats with a 1-1 home draw against our Essex visitors. But there were mixed feelings after Josh Sheehan gave us an early lead only for Colchester to level from the penalty spot.

Westley found a new way of attempting to inspire us in the dressing room the following Saturday before a crucial away game at Barnet. This time he turned to Al Pacino and his famous speech from *Any Given Sunday,* including the message: "It all comes down to today. Either we heal as a team or we are going to crumble, inch by inch, play by play, til we're finished and get the shit kicked out of us or we can fight our way back into the light." The result was a hard earned 0-0 draw with the manager insisting afterwards that, before we became a winning side, we had to be an unbeaten one.

The win that we all craved wasn't too long in coming, as Westley again used the motivational words of Al Pacino before Ryan Bird scored once and got an assist against his former club as we defeated fellow strugglers Hartlepool United 3-1 at home. That temporarily closed the gap to safety to three points but, although we eventually stretched our unbeaten run to six games, we finished that run a further point adrift.

The clash with leaders Doncaster Rovers at home on a Friday night under the floodlights was always going to be a big challenge and this was the first time the manager took over the music in the dressing room. He played random stuff starting with Boney M's *Daddy Kool* and *Best in Me* by Blue before sending us out to face Donny with *Who Let the Dogs Out?* The manager explained the stories behind each song, the last one being obvious.

As the referee banged on the door and the dogs of war emerged, I admit to feeling a little embarrassed. We then put in a big physical effort to earn ourselves a deserved point from another 0-0 draw. That was a good result although a win would have hauled us out of the relegation zone.

Normal practice would be to have a couple of days rest or a light cooling down session with another home match on the Tuesday night, but the manager had other ideas. He had us in on the Saturday morning doing 500 reps in the gym during a gruelling upper body session. Ok, this meant less strain on our legs but bodies and minds in the group were becoming tired.

There was no point talking to Graham Westley about that – he wasn't that kind of manager. Had any of us said that we were knackered, he'd have taken that as a sign of weakness. Something wrong perhaps in our personal recovery programmes?

Tiredness may have played a part in our 3-2 defeat at Cambridge United after two Ryan Bird goals gave us a 2-0 lead. Certainly, we faded late in the match as the home side drew level, then got the winner from a controversial penalty.

A few of us voiced how we were feeling back in training after the following weekend's 1-1 draw with Morecambe. Fellow centre back Darren Jones said his legs were killing him and left back Dan Butler, who hadn't been in the team for a while, said something similar, despite being known as a very fit lad. My body told me the same thing.

In came Graham Westley and asked the lads how they were. When Darren said his legs felt stiff, the manager queried if he was looking after himself properly. Then I admitted that I was below my best. When it came to Dan's turn, he shocked us all by telling the boss he was as 'fit as a fiddle'. That made us laugh afterwards. Dan said he'd been out of the team long enough and was happy to lie his way back into the manager's plans. We all understood his point.

Defeat at Mansfield followed when the manager ran the gauntlet of unhappy supporters, before we hosted a must-win home game against a Leyton Orient side alongside us in the relegation zone.

In my opinion, that was the afternoon when all of our chickens came back to roost. Constant football Tuesday, Saturday, Tuesday with gruelling training sessions in between left us with precious little in the tank. And a young Orient, containing several teenagers, ran us off our feet. We were 2-0 down inside the opening 13 minutes and it went from bad to worse. My day was complete when I conceded a second half penalty as the visitors ran out convincing 4-0 winners.

That was Graham Westley's last game in charge of Newport County. We'd gone seven matches without a win during a very important stage of the season and were marooned 11 points behind Notts County who occupied the spot just above the drop zone.

Family is everything to me.

I still keep in touch with my mates back home in Ireland.

It was always a proud moment to represent my country in the famous green shirt.

Making my debut for Derby against Watford on 3 May 2009. I was just 16.

Robbie Savage was the first to pat me on the back and say 'well done'.

Although we lost 3-1, which was disappointing, we didn't concede whilst I was on the pitch.

Derby County v Nottingham Forest is a huge game.
I had no idea of the intensity of the rivalry until I experienced it for myself.

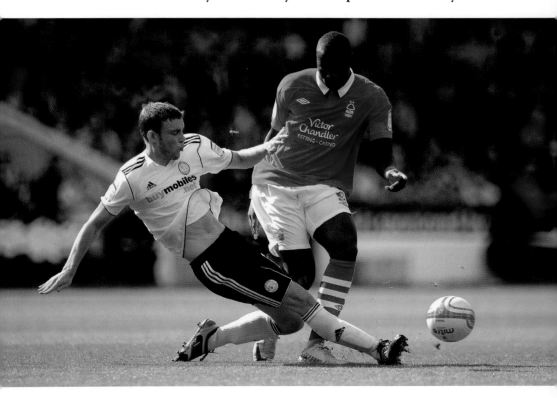

I relished my physical battle with Forest's Ishmael Miller
at the City Ground in September 2011.

Here I am heading the ball away from Nottingham Forest's Wes Morgan, Luke Chambers and goalkeeper Lee Camp in our 2-1 victory over Forest in September 2011.

Beating Forest is always good, but victory also meant that we won the Brian Clough trophy

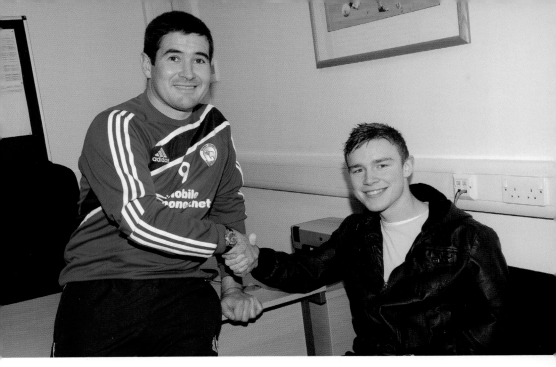

I'm eternally grateful to Nigel Clough for giving me my big break whilst at Derby.

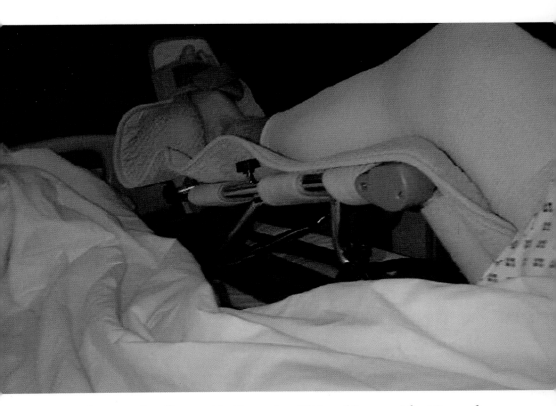

I injured my cruciate ligament in December 2011 and I was out for 10 months.

Playing for Motherwell against Celtic at Celtic park was a dream come true.

My committed style of play meant I suffered multiple head injuries.

I had high expectations when I joined Luton Town in 2015, but my spell at Kenilworth Road left me feeling that I was at rock bottom.

Luton Town physio Simon Parselle was a massive help to me during what was a very difficult time. I always look forward to seeing him.

I spent two loan spells at Southport where I scored my first professional goal.

Enjoying a night out with Jeff Hendrick and his pals.

My Luton teammate Paddy McCourt invited me to spend Christmas with his family during my time at Kenilworth Road.

After leaving Luton in January 2017, I signed for Newport County. At the time, I didn't even know Newport was in Wales!

In modern football nobody was too surprised by the sacking. But I had mixed feelings. I saw that Westley tried everything possible to lift us. Similar methods worked at Stevenage but, for whatever reason, it didn't happen for Newport. True to form, he texted us all individually after the announcement and wished us well.

No sane person would have put their mortgage on Newport staying in the EFL that Saturday night. We were significantly worse off than when Westley took over from Warren Feeney and there were only 12 matches left. We needed a miracle but, for me, giving up wasn't an option. Where the club was heading was more important, but my personal future was also firmly on the line.

CHAPTER FIVE
MARK O'BRIEN DAY

By MICHAEL FLYNN, Newport County manager 2017-2021

I KNEW what I was getting in Mark O'Brien, the footballer, when I came in as manager as the last throw of the dice by Newport in March 2017.

I'd been on the coaching staff under Graham Westley and played in a couple of reserve games with Mark. Pardon the pun, but he was a wholehearted defender, always prepared to put his body on the line and would never pull out of a challenge, even if it was 70-30 against him.

Mark wrote his name into Newport folklore that day a couple of months later. For seven or eight minutes, we were getting relegated and, as a Newport lad, I was feeling sorry for the fans because I knew what it meant to them. I was trying to think of different things to do, including possibly one last substitution, when Mark waved to the bench for permission to go forward.

In a way, his goal was straight off the training ground. Mark and Joss Labadie used to practice controlling the ball on the chest and volleying and it felt like muscle memory when Mark scored that late, late goal that clinched our 'great escape'. It was a moment that we'll never forget for the rest of our lives.

*****

I DIDN'T know anything about the club's history when I joined. In fact when Newport was first mentioned to me, I asked: "Which part of England is that in?" I honestly had no idea that I was heading for South Wales!

But I discovered later why all Newport followers view relegation from the Football League with dread – it's happened before and that was nearly the end of football in the town.

It all happened in the rollercoaster 1980s – a decade before I was born. They started so well with Newport winning the Welsh Cup and a place in the European Cup Winners' Cup in 1980/81. That's when they really started to create club history.

Crusaders, of Northern Ireland, and Norway's SK Hagar were thrashed 4-0 and 6-0 respectively at our old Somerton Park Ground. That, remarkably, took Newport into the last eight of a major European competition – and it nearly got even better. Tommy Tynan scored both goals as we held East German giants Carl Zeiss Jena to a 2-2 draw in the away leg. The ground was packed with more than 18,000 fans for the return game which Newport reportedly dominated before eventually losing 1-0.

That denied us the chance of playing an even bigger European name in Portugal's Benfica in the semi-finals, whilst the East Germans went on to reach the final, losing to Dinamo Tbilisi, of the former Soviet Union.

Under Colin Addison, a very successful Newport manager who'd previously plotted a 'great escape' from relegation out of the Football League in the 1970s, the club then went from strength to strength.

In 1982/3 a fourth placed finish in the Third Division was the highest position the club had achieved since the Second World War. We finished only four points behind promoted Huddersfield Town, having topped the table as near the end as April after a 1-0 win over Welsh rivals Cardiff City in front of more than 16,000 fans.

There were other memorable cup days, including holding Everton, one of the top sides in the country, 1-1 in the FA Cup before going out 2-1 at Goodison Park and reaching another Welsh Cup final in 1987 in which Merthyr Tydfil triumphed after a replay. Then it all went wrong – big time wrong. That same season in which we reached the Welsh Cup final ended in relegation from Division Three and 12 months later came the worst blow of all as Newport ended up rock bottom of Division Four with just 25 points.

That was a disaster. Not just because it ended a proud 60-year stay in the Football League but because our very existence was in grave danger.

Followers of today's National League will be familiar with Wrexham's astonishing story when, under their Hollywood owners and all the global publicity that has generated, they blasted their way back into the EFL in 2022/23 But, for every glory ride like that, there are horror stories – clubs who strive for years and years, like Wrexham before their change of ownership, to get their old status back and sometimes fall even lower.

Newport never finished that first season in the old Conference and by the end of February 1989 had officially gone out of business with debts of £330,000. That looked like the end but never underestimate our ever-loyal fans. Newport AFC was formed a few months later by club chairman, David Hando, and 400 supporters, beginning life in the Hellenic League, four levels below the EFL.

There were more than football obstacles to climb on the way back. Newport Council refused the club permission to return to Somerton Park because of unpaid rent and instead, the club played their first home matches in Gloucestershire at Moreton -in-Marsh, a full 80 miles away from Newport. This was how the club got its present nickname of The Exiles as we were not wanted in Wales because we played in the English League.

The new League of Wales wanted Newport to join, but we fought on, including a spell at Gloucester City's Meadow Park stadium, before a High Court decision allowed us to move to the newly built Newport Stadium.

Getting back into the EFL itself proved a very long journey. Even storming through the Southern Midland League by a 14-point margin proved a false dawn as Newport then suffered a further relegation.

It took until the 2004-5 season to reach Conference South and another five years to get out of it – with a record 105 points total and after Newport had won one and lost two Football Association of Wales cup finals. Still the job wasn't done – the sworn mission of the newly-formed club was to get back into the EFL.

The late and much missed Justin Edinburgh's first task in charge at Newport was to win a relegation battle and there was the heartbreak of a 2-0 defeat in the play-off final by York

City before, by then at Rodney Parade, we finally reached the promised land via the 2013 Conference play-off final.

That was a truly historic occasion as two Welsh sides battled it out at Wembley for the first time ever and we came out on top against Wrexham. Wounds with the local authority were healed as promotion won the club the freedom of Newport. That's just a short history but it's impossible to do justice to how important being in the EFL is to Newport people.

Little did I know it – and I'm very pleased that I was in the dark – the consequences of Newport being relegated again during my first season there would have gone far beyond football. There were plenty of folk still associated with the club who remembered the story I have just written because they were there. Some lost their jobs; others their passion.

Bigger football clubs can be confident of overcoming the loss of funding that comes from losing their status. Behind the scenes, our club was desperately worried that history was about to repeat itself – and this time there might be no way back.

One of the keys to our subsequent revival and survival was that ignorance can truly be bliss and we just got on with the job.

People ask what changed from a side marooned at the bottom of Division Four to the one that miraculously clawed its way to safety in the last few minutes of the last day. The honest answer is very little. And it was helpful keeping ourselves under the radar, concentrating on our jobs and not thinking about the wider implications.

The first issue was who was going to take over. In my relatively short career, I discovered at both Derby County and Luton Town how large an impact a new manager could have on my career. I did well during my first few games at Newport but what importance would a new manager coming in from elsewhere put on that? Particularly when it looked as if changes were urgently needed.

I only had the security of a deal and wage until the last day of the season and, after so long out in the cold, it would have been heart-breaking had my chance to help Newport ended there and then. So, yes, I was quietly pleased when it was announced that Michael Flynn, one of the coaches under Graham Westley, was taking caretaker charge until the end of the season.

Flynny is a local lad, who had four spells with Newport as a player, and knew the club inside out. He saw how hard I'd worked in training and my performances on the pitch. We seemed to get on well. Nevertheless, I was very relieved when I saw my name on the teamsheet for his first game.

Personnel-wise and in terms of tactics, Flynn didn't change an awful lot. But the impact he made on us as a group was major. The main thing he did was relax us, taking away the physical and mental pressure that we'd been used to.

Whereas Graham Westley worked us into the ground, Flynn wanted us fresh and fit for the games. There was instantly a better atmosphere around the first team and a feeling we had nothing to lose.

I think it was beneficial that the players were all familiar with him. For much of that season the boss had been one of us – a player. I'd played alongside him, both as a defender and a midfielder, as well as knowing him as a coach.

Flynn was Newport through and through and added to that feeling by appointing former Exile Wayne Hatswell as his assistant. It was as if we'd put the 'Newport' back into the club – warts and all. And we were all on the same page.

When you've got a mountain to climb, there's only one place to start – the first step. That was a trip to Crewe Alexandra on the Saturday.

Things didn't start well. We were deservedly 1-0 down at half time and the sight of Flynn shouting instructions from the touchline was confusing. Until recently one of us, now he was telling us what to do.

To make things worse, we struggled defensively. We didn't know whether to back off to defend their long balls forward or squeeze and press them. We were getting both instructions from the touchline and I wasn't happy. When we stopped for a drinks break with us still 1-0 down, I let off some steam. "What the f--- do you want us to do? We can't do both," I barked at Flynn.

Had he not been so familiar, I wouldn't' have spoken to him like that. It still hadn't quite clicked that now he was the one in charge. To his credit, he dealt with me without any drama. He urged us to relax and defend properly and emphasised that we were still very much in the game. And so it proved. Dan Butler volleyed in the equaliser, then after 89 minutes Joss Labadie grabbed the winner.

Wow, what a feeling! Flynn said that he could see the smiles on the boys' faces and he was right. Victory probably surprised us a little, to be honest, but was a perfect start. The winner coming right at the end was the icing on the cake. Game by game, our mission was do everything possible to get three points, then move on. No time to feel sorry for ourselves, we needed to close the gap on our relegation rivals step by step.

We were back in action again the following Tuesday at Morecambe. They were doing quite well in mid-table and it was asking a lot for us to pull off a second away win in succession.

But that's exactly what we did! With the game still scoreless midway through the second half, Alex Samuel was felled in the penalty area and Ryan Bird stepped up to convert the spot kick. Two wins out of two, fantastic! A few short days ago we'd been 11 points from safety, suddenly the gap was down to seven.

But, if anyone thought we'd cracked it, we were brought back down to earth instantly. We'd looked forward to Flynny's first game at Rodney Parade and were confident of making it a hat trick of wins even though Blackpool were pushing for the play offs.

Yet this wasn't our day. We conceded a poor goal early on and only the woodwork prevented it being two or three. Alex Samuel bundled in a goal with 15 minutes to bring us back to 2-1, but that was as good as it got. Blackpool scored again to clinch the points. This survival mission was never going to be straightforward.

They say treat victory and defeat much the same way – don't get too high when you win, don't get too down in the dumps when you lose. That's how we approached it. No point kicking ourselves or conducting an inquest. Flynn told us to forget Blackpool and move on. That proved an effective policy.

The manager took the stress out of our football lives. Everything became fun again. We enjoyed ourselves in training and came together on a Saturday physically less tired and mentally ready. Only our most loyal fans thought there was any chance of Newport County staying up, so our results went largely unnoticed. That was the way we liked it.

Nevertheless, our midweek home game against Luton Town

inevitably brought me into the limelight a little. My unhappy spell at Kenilworth Road had ended earlier that same season so it was inevitable that the local media would write about me wanting to prove a point against my former employers.

They were right. Every game was vital but, because of my unhappy times there, Luton's visit added extra spice. I was desperate to play well and show Nathan Jones and their fans, social media critics included, that I was a very good player at this level.

My mate Alan Sheehan was in the Luton side and it looked ominous when one of their big hitters, Danny Hylton, put them ahead as early as the fifth minute from a penalty. But Sean Rigg got us back into the game before the half hour and we gave as good as we got against a Luton side riding high in the play offs.

Even getting sent off in the 89th minute for a second of two late yellow cards didn't take away the fact that I had been on top of my game. A 1-1 draw was a point on the board for us and a point made by me. Luton would have been very disappointed not to beat us.

The positive reaction I got afterwards was an extra bonus. Many of the lads shook my hand to say how well I'd done. It was the same with the Luton coaching staff as well – bar one!

That was Nathan Jones. The fact that he didn't shake my hand was further vindication in my view. He saw what his colleagues thought of me, yet he was the one who refused to play me for Luton Town. That night was another step in my rehabilitation post Kenilworth Road.

Unfortunately, the red card meant a one match ban, so I was in the stand rather than on the pitch when we travelled to Pompey at the weekend. This was a big ask against a side in the automatic promotion places and so it proved. We thought we should have had a penalty in the first half before we went 2-0 down and were left with a mountain to climb. Alex Samuel's goal set up a frantic finish but a 2-1 scoreline meant that we had no points to show despite a creditable showing.

We were inevitably looking at the results of fellow relegation contenders. Leyton Orient's defeat meant that we stayed one point above them at the bottom. Meanwhile Cheltenham and Hartlepool, six and eight points above us respectively, also lost away from home – results that took the edge off what could have been a very costly defeat for us.

We desperately needed to make home advantage count on April Fool's Day against Crawley and, thanks to a long-range special from my defensive colleague and mate Mickey Demetriou, we did just that. It was a nervy old finish though after Joss Labadie and one of their lads had been red carded just after half time.

That meant we travelled to Exeter City in good spirits and what happened there, in my opinion, proved a major turning point in our eventual survival. This was a three-hour trip at the best of times but we got badly stuck in traffic and started to panic. At 2.30pm, just half an hour before kick off, we were stuck on the motorway and not going to make it on time.

Our kit man was already at the ground, so we got messages to him whilst Michael Flynn told us to go on social media and spread word about our predicament.

This tale highlights one of the differences between football in the top two divisions and lower down. It's unthinkable that Manchester United would be late for a game because their travel arrangements are far different.

We were in big trouble. In our position in the league, we couldn't afford an off day. Perhaps it would be better if we didn't play at all?

When a postponement was becoming a real possibility, the traffic suddenly cleared all at once. It was like the parting of the Red Sea on the motorway and we got to the ground without any further problems at 3.30pm. The referee warned us that we had only 15 minutes because he wanted to kick off at 3.45pm. So, we got changed, came out for a couple of moments to jog onto the pitch and went straight into battle.

Our distress probably galvanised us. Also, we knew how our rivals were faring. After doing well to keep our game scoreless at the break, we found out both Hartlepool and Cheltenham had drawn.

Somehow, we had to win to close the gap. Our big break came in the 53rd minute when Tom Owen-Evans got the ball in midfield, took a touch and slammed a long range shot into the bottom corner. It could have been 2-0 moments later when Alex Samuel shot just over, but we were forced to batten down the hatches in the closing stages as Exeter threw everything at us to attempt to rescue at least a draw.

If any game gave us belief that we could escape relegation, it was that traumatic afternoon in Exeter. Everything was against us. Nobody would have been remotely surprised had we got beaten. Yet, despite facing a home team and crowd baying for blood, we got three points!

That was the best feeling ever. We celebrated to the song *Ain't No Stopping Us Now*. That perfectly summed up how our very tired group of players thought after a Saturday that we'll never forget. Two wins on the bounce, three points from safety. Game on!

Seven days later, two wins became three and again demon defender Mickey Demetriou was the toast of Newport. A larger than usual crowd of around 3,700 gathered at an expectant Rodney Parade as word began to get round about our revival. Also, visitors Yeovil were by no means safe themselves. Mickey struck a spectacular winner from a free kick for the only goal.

Eyes turned to the updated league table – four games to go and we were only a single point behind Hartlepool with Leyton Orient all but dead and buried at the bottom. Suddenly we believed that anything was possible. Yes, we could go to title chasing Plymouth Argyle and beat them on their own patch the following Saturday. Why not? We were on a roll with confidence as high as it had been all season. Pressure was on the home side as a win could clinch promotion to League One.

Instead, we got thumped by a very good attacking side. Plymouth won 6-1 – no good at all for our goal difference. Two goals at the end of the first half gave us a mountain to climb and, when you go a few behind to a good side on their own pitch, it can get ugly.

After defeats like that, you need good man management – and we got it. The vastly experienced Lenny Lawrence, who was helping our management duo, came into the dressing room to say it was just one game and to forget it. That made more sense than extra training or going over a disastrous afternoon with a fine toothcomb, as could have happened previously.

Players know when they haven't performed well. They don't need to relive it time and again by being shown the horror video. We didn't go out that night but were given the right message: heads high, remember how well we'd done to give us a chance of staying up and prepare for the next game. Everyone knows getting thrashed can sap your confidence for the next game. We didn't have time to let that happen. And there was one major consolation – Hartlepool lost.

The fans again turned out in force for the following weekend's home game against play off hunting Accrington Stanley and enjoyed an afternoon to savour. Unbelievably, after being 11 points adrift a few weeks before, we moved out of the relegation zone altogether when Ryan Bird headed the only goal from point blank range. Another defeat for Hartlepool meant that we were now two points above them. So, victory at Carlisle, a side just outside the promotion zone, could see us get the job done with a match to spare.

That was when the national media started to take notice. After going unnoticed and unreported for so long, they hit on the unlikely story of a 'great escape'. They drew parallels with Colin Addison's side in the 1970s and were seemingly willing us on to do the same. That was great but it also cranked up the pressure. We honestly preferred it when we were in our own bubble.

A rollercoaster afternoon started with everything going to plan. Mickey Demetriou struck yet again with a superb header and a few minutes later Cheltenham, not totally out of the woods themselves, hit the front against Pool. With those scores remaining unchanged until half time, we were, in theory, only 45 minutes away from safety.

It's one thing chasing sides above you and having the blood chasing around your veins. To get over the line when you are in front is another matter. And, in all honesty, the signs of what was to come were there. We'd defended cross after cross; goalkeeper Joe Day had made saves and they'd missed chances.

Was it asking too much for our luck to hold? The answer was 'yes' as they hit us with a double strike around the hour mark and we couldn't get back into the game. At least Pool lost, so our destiny remained in our own hands going into the last matchday of the season.

This guaranteed another seven days of media attention. It was always going to be a long build up to our final game against Notts County at Rodney Parade with the destiny of the whole season – and maybe the club itself – riding on the outcome.

A GAME OF TWO HEARTS

You can tell yourself a thousand times 'it's just another game of football'. Try that when you've been fighting for nine or ten months and the outcome rests on the last 90 minutes! Notts County was our cup final – and we knew it.

You can't help but go through every possibility: we could lose and stay up but, as Pool had a one goal better goal difference, we could draw and get relegated.

Mike Flynn and Wayne Hatswell did a great job taking the pressure off the players by handling all the media interviews. They wanted us to view the game as business as usual.

There'd been very few changes during their tumultuous few weeks in charge. We lined up 3-5-2 with the players that they trusted and we gave it everything. The media looked for Flynn's secret formula for success but there wasn't one. The management trusted us to do our jobs on the pitch and gave us the right backing. There were no special tactics.

On the Friday before the big game, I was with Mickey Demetriou in the hotel that we had been put in since my arrival at Newport. He was up there as probably my best centre back partner and we'd got to know each other as friends. We did our best to occupy ourselves and keep calm.

There was another complication about the last day – and the media were involved in that too. All League Two games kicked off at the same time at 5.20pm instead of the usual 3pm. Having an extra two hours to kick when our football body clocks were set for 3pm only added to the almost unbearable tension.

I woke up at about 9am, a full eight hours or more before the game. And, despite going through everything that I thought could happen, nothing prepared me for what did.

Dad asked me how I was feeling. "Fine, Dad," I said. "But a bit nervous." That was an understatement! "It's only another game of ball," he said. Oh no, not that phrase again! But the thought was a good one. I was going to ring him again when I got to the stadium, but he said no. That's when I discovered even he could be superstitious. "You didn't phone the last two games when you won. Let's keep it the same – ring me afterwards," he suggested.

Ok, fine. My phone was on silent for much of the day. I appreciated the many well-wishers but looking at messages only added to the tension. I knew how nervous I was because I didn't eat much that match day – the butterflies in my stomach saw to that!

The biggest thing in our favour was our home crowd. Rodney Parade was sold out for the first and only time all season with the vast majority of the 7,300-plus backing us every inch of the way.

Sat in the dressing room before kick off, *Ain't No Stopping Us Now* was played over the tannoy system. We liked that. It had become our unofficial theme tune, post Exeter.

Rodney Parade was excitable but nervous. Notts were beatable having been part of the relegation battle for several months. But they'd proved a sterner proposition under new manager Kevin Nolan and were now happily safe.

Lannell John-Lewis, recently returned to the starting line-up after being injured in a pre-season friendly, was again in the side. At least he was one person who hadn't gone through much of the tension of the last few months.

Predictably most of the game was a blur. They tell me big Jon Stead went close for them in the early stages, but the first moment I recall was John-Lewis being brought down in their penalty area.

It could only be man of the moment – metal Mickey – to take the all-important spot kick. Voted League 2 player of the month for April, he stepped up to smash the ball into the Notts County net and send Rodney Parade wild with delight. At the interval we were 1-0 up and Pool were trailing by the same score to Doncaster Rovers. Anyone taking anything for granted only had to go back seven days!

Usually, we were good at protecting 1-0 leads and the second half started with us looking in control. That lasted until the 61st minute when, in an innocuous looking Notts attack, Mickey went into a tackle, the ball ricocheted off my knee and let in Jorge Grant for the equaliser.

Immediately, you could sense the change in atmosphere in the stadium – excitement to very flat. We had to lift ourselves and bag a winner or our fate depended on Pool.

For a while we knew that they were still losing 1-0 but then came the news we were dreading. Pool scored after 74 minutes and, worse still, nine minutes later they went 2-1 ahead! From being five points clear in the minute-by-minute league table, yet again we were staring relegation in the face.

Pressure was on us to get the ball forward quickly. We were rushing and panicking with minutes seemingly ticking ever faster. It must have been 87 or 88 minutes when I signalled to the bench for permission to go forward. It was a tactic we'd used before – throw me up front to try to win a flick on, cause an issue in their minds. Never mind I'd never scored.

Michael Flynn said 'no'. Wayne said 'yes'. I went with the latter. What happened next blows my mind even now.

Joss Labadie played a great pass to David Pipe who, for once, took the ball on his left foot and crossed. Marlon Jackson and Ryan Bird were standing in front of me. Marlon flicked the ball on and it came towards me at the far post. Instinctively I controlled the ball on my chest so I could volley it, connected as hard as I could with my right foot and watched as it headed for the bottom corner.

I ran and ran. People ask me about my celebration, but I had no idea what I was doing. I was completely taken over by the moment. Dan Butler gave me a playful nudge and I went sprawling to the ground with Newport players climbing onto my back. Flairs were thrown onto the pitch, fans kicked advertising boards.

It was mayhem, chaos! But we still needed to keep our heads. The board came up with five minutes of added time. Five minutes? That can seem a long time.

We took no chances. Five at the back, three just in front. Somehow Marlon Jackson must have kept the ball in the corner for three of those minutes. Former England player Alan Smith did his best to rally Notts. "Let's get a goal, relegate Newport!" he roared. It felt like us against the world. Ok, let's admit it, we weren't the most popular team in League Two.

We'd used that thought to our advantage over the last few months – could we do so now for just a couple of minutes? There was one last goal kick for Notts. We'd played six or seven extra minutes. Mickey Demetriou headed the ball into touch, Josh Labadie won one final ball in the air and, finally, it was all over!

The whistle meant salvation for Newport and the best feeling of my football life. When the manager came into the dressing room, we were singing and dancing 'we are staying up, we are staying up!' The mood and the tune didn't change much all night.

I was sat next to goalkeeper Joe Day who asked who scored the winning goal. He honestly didn't know! "I scored it, it was me!" I said.

"F--- off," he said, thinking I was joking.

I don't blame him. I could hardly believe it myself. It was my first ever goal in the EFL, my other goal in professional football coming for Southport. There could not have been a more unlikely goal scorer bar Jimmy Glass, the Carlisle goalkeeper, who famously came up for a last minute corner to keep his side in the league. When he realised the truth, Joe gave me a big, big hug!

I've been through a lot in my career in football, highs and devastating lows, but that was the only time I cried on a football pitch. It was so emotional and has done so much to help the club in the next few years.

Much credit must go to Michael Flynn who got us all singing from the same hymn sheet and believing that we could achieve the near impossible. But I'd also like to thank Graham Westley. He couldn't get the best out of us but put his faith in me and helped to get me fit.

My interview with BBC Wales on the pitch after the game touched on the fact that my personal future was still in the air. That was neither the time nor place to think about me. That time would come.

We went out on the town and were given a great reception by Newport folk as we sung 'we are staying up', climbed on chairs and tables and generally let our hair down. That was the kind of feeling you play football all your life for. And, yes, I'd dreamt of having my moment, having watched iconic goals such as Aguero winning the Premier League for Manchester City and Robbie Brady heading a last minute winner for the Republic.

There and then it happened. I was the toast of Newport County having scored a goal that meant so much to the players, the club, the whole place.

Having gone through a lot of things in my young life on and off the field, I felt that this was my reward. Somehow, even my winning goal was meant to be, so I could kick on and put the past behind me.

After the high tension and excitement of such an important match and the celebrations that followed, I needed instead to get away from football and have a rest.

Everything seemed to be coming together. I had a club and team I wanted to play for. Newport was my new Derby. A place I could again call home and enjoy my football. I was both liked and wanted.

Now I could rebuild my career without feeling on the edge. I had a manager who had faith in me, rather than being one mistake away from being discarded.

They still call May 6 Mark O'Brien Day in that part of Wales in my honour – and I love it!

My future was secondary to the club's, but I would have been forced to pack my bags and leave Newport behind if Hartlepool had stayed up instead of us.

Many who have come to Newport, either permanently or on loan, have caught the bug and realised what a passionate footballing place this is. I am certainly one of those!

It only struck me fully in the weeks afterwards exactly how much that incredible day meant to the people. I remain very proud to have been part of it.

CHAPTER SIX
GIANT KILLINGS AND KNOCKING ON PROMOTION DOOR

By MICHAEL FLYNN, former Newport County manager

We went on to have some great times in both the FA Cup and the league after escaping relegation and Mark played a big part.

We have a laugh about it now, but I'll always remember getting very excited after taking a phone call saying that Ben White was available for the Spurs replay at Wembley, without thinking that it was Mark who was missing out. Yet it was so typical of Mark that he came on towards the end of the game and gave his all.

Then Mark blamed himself for us not getting promoted at Wembley after his sending off when, without him, we wouldn't have got anywhere near that stage.

A few things went against us in the play off final against Tranmere, including a stonewall penalty decision. It was just not meant to be.

*****

NO MATTER who came in for me that summer – Manchester United, Real Madrid or anyone – I was always going to sign for Newport County.

The manner of our great escape left me and Newport on a real high and I'd totally bought into what I consider to be a unique football club. So, I was itching to find out how far we could go and looking to fully re-establish myself by playing week in week out.

What followed was a successful 2017/18 season for the club, but an up and down time for me as I again battled injury and was in and out of the starting eleven.

First things first, I needed a holiday – a total break from football and I got one. Mike Flynn promised not to phone, text or contact me in any way for a couple of weeks if I gave my word that I would sign my contract. Done Deal!

I returned to Dublin to see family and friends delighted that I'd put my Luton nightmare behind me. They were pleased about 'that goal', Newport's survival and that I had a two-year contract waiting for me.

My mate Jeff Hendrick, by this time playing Premier League football with Burnley, invited me over to Marbella for a few days. Party time! A long weekend with Jeff and the lads was the perfect way to wind down after our emotional and physical rollercoaster.

I was delighted to hear Jeff's news and how well his career was progressing as we renewed the friendship that we'd enjoyed since our Republic of Ireland age group days. There was laughter, drink and not much sleep. For a few days, football wasn't the be all and end all.

Yet, much to my surprise, we bumped into not one, not two, but THREE Newport players on that break. Joss Labadie, Tom Owen-Evans and Jazzi Barnum-Bobb were also in Spain letting their hair down, so we joined forces to further celebrate our success.

More Dublin time followed and, at the end of the curfew, Mike Flynn phoned to make the contract offer official and I agreed on the spot – two more years at Newport sounded great.

My mate Mickey Demetriou was also on the phone – and I couldn't get him off it! He had found an apartment and would I like to share it with him? That was an easy decision because we got on so well, on and off the field, but that was only the beginning of the story for Mickey.

I sent him my first month's rent and trusted him completely, but he was constantly in touch about buying this or that for our new pad. My answer was always 'go and do it'. The differences in our personalities were becoming more obvious.

I found Mickey difficult to live with in some ways because

he is very particular and has his superstitions. This wasn't a real problem because we had already come to know each other well and rubbed along just fine. Amusingly, we were often described in banter by teammates as 'like a married couple'. That was taken in good fun, even by Mickey's real partner who was living back home.

Mickey's pre-match routine never changed. On a Friday, he ate pesto pasta and chicken. Always the same and only the one version. I'd have gladly eaten anything he cooked! We also played Mario Kart on the Wii console throughout our year together – no matter that he only beat me a handful of times!

Another example of Mickey's attention for detail was when he returned home to see his fiancée, now wife, for a few days, leaving me in charge of domestic affairs. I put all the crockery in the dishwasher and faced an inquisition when Mickey returned. "What did you do with my Costa glass cups?" he asked. These were the ones he used to brew up his favourite hot chocolate.

When I said that I'd put them in the dishwasher with the rest of the pots, he claimed that I shouldn't have done so because 'they'd come out a different shade of glass'. This added another dimension to our banter!

Back to football, I was wondering what Mike Flynn's pre-season training would be like. I was a confirmed hater of this part of the football season, but half of me thought, because he'd introduced a more relaxed approach after Graham Westley's departure, his regime might be more to my taste.

Wrong! Mike and Wayne were proper old school with the first few weeks consisting of running, running and more running. Starting with a run around the track, followed by another four! Then we were doing four 1000m runs and four 800m runs in the same session.

For three or four weeks, it was pure hell and I suffered most. At previous clubs where we were put through the mill fitness-wise, there were usually three groups – very good runners, ok winners and slow coaches, including me! Now I was in a group all on my own. I'd be lapped and mocked. Nothing that I could do to avoid it!

It did my head in as I couldn't reconcile all the running with what happens on the pitch. Still don't to a degree. Constant running seemed over the top as we only get the ball out after three or four weeks.

But I knew that our management duo wanted us to be fitter than our opponents and their policy was justified when we made a good start to the season. We were 3-1 down on opening day at Stevenage but had enough in our legs, as well as the ability, to draw 3-3.

To their credit, the managers stayed true to their values and what made Newport special. Signings were made for character as well as talent. Flynny saw how a bunch of misfits had pulled us through the previous season. Many of us had struggled elsewhere or were coming back from injury, yet we revelled as underdogs at Newport.

We didn't know how far we could go in the league after beating the drop in the most dramatic and uplifting of circumstances but we were excited to find out.

Our immediate task was made more difficult as 'fortress' Rodney Parade wasn't available until the end of August after the pitch had been re-laid during the summer. That meant playing our opening three League Two matches – and five in all competitions – away.

Five points from three games, including a notable 1-0 victory in our first ever visit to Coventry City's Ricoh Arena, was very good and there was the bonus of winning 2-0 at League One Southend United in the first round of the EFL Cup. That meant a big second round trip to Elland Road to face a Leeds United side destined to play a significant role in our season.

I'd briefly tasted the atmosphere of this famous ground when being on the bench for Derby County, so I knew something of what to expect.

Skipper Joss Labadie gave us a first half lead and we were well in contention to pull off a shock before Kemar Roofe equalised just before the break. It was all downhill afterwards as Roofe completed his hat trick and Leeds went on to win 5-1.

Naturally we were disappointed to be on the receiving end of what looked like a hiding but felt that the scoreline was harsh. Nearly every time the home side had a chance, they scored. The main difference was the quality of their forwards, but we also played some good football.

There was more pressure on us to perform when we finally walked out at Rodney Parade for the first time since that historic victory over Notts County. It wasn't the easiest of challenges when Chesterfield visited a few days after the Leeds tie, but we responded in style after going in at half time a goal down. Frank Nouble helped himself to a hat trick as we christened our lovely new playing surface with a 4-1 victory. Eight points from four points lifted us into second place, but I suffered a setback as I had to come off after an hour.

That was the start of a foot injury that frustrated me for much of that season. Medics couldn't shed too much light on the injury, but it was enough to sideline me for several games and needed careful management. For weeks, I didn't train but played on the Saturday as wearing insoles in my boots eventually improved things.

The way that the season progressed the FA Cup became particularly important to us, but that wasn't by design. Our attitude was to give it 100 per cent in all competitions and obviously our great start raised hopes that we could challenge for promotion in the league.

The only competition in which Flynn significantly changed the side was the EFL Trophy in which League One and League Two clubs are mostly joined by Premier League Under 21 sides. We didn't play down the importance of the event as it provides lower league teams with their one realistic chance of getting to Wembley. But, in the early rounds, it made sense to give young and fringe players their chance. I wasn't much involved as we lost to Forest Green, Swansea City Under 21s and Cheltenham.

In stark contrast, a famous FA Cup run began with a 2-1 home victory over Walsall, a cup shock as they were League One, but one that didn't register outside of Newport. This was one early game in which I got a view of future England international Ben White, who joined us on loan from Brighton for the season. I played alongside him and Mickey Demetriou in a back three that afternoon as he began to settle into the side.

My first impression of the teenager was that he was naturally composed and talented on the ball, but I didn't know how he would cope with the physical demands of League Two football. He was sent to Newport to mature as a player and a person and I saw his progress during the season.

Ben played a starring role in Arsenal's magnificent 2022/23 season in the Premier League in which they eventually missed out on the title to Manchester City. And he was also selected for England's World Cup squad in Qatar.

I did my best to help him even when he was picked in front of me – there's an interesting story about the Tottenham cup tie to come! In those situations, you either get defensive or play your role for the team. I never hoped someone would play shit, so that I could walk back into the side. I wanted every Newport player to succeed for the good of the club.

The luck of the draw gave us four home FA Cup ties as we created history by reaching the fourth round. Next up after Walsall were Cambridge United who were in the same division. Not the most glamorous of ties but one that gave us a 50-50 chance of getting through to the third round when the big boys from the Premier League and the Championship enter the competition. Joss Labadie scored twice as our name went into the hat and two weeks later tormented Cambridge again in a league game that was particularly important for different reasons.

We knew as we travelled to Cambridge, that we'd be flying out straight afterwards for our Christmas party. To ensure that the weekend went with a swing, we needed to get our job done before letting our hair down. Keen to avenge their FA Cup exit, Cambridge gave us a very good game. When they equalised midway through the second half, we were under pressure to avoid defeat before Labadie came up with an unusual way of getting the party started. They say it doesn't matter how you score – whether it goes in off your backside or flies into the top corner from 30 yards. This was more like the former! The Cambridge goalkeeper made a panicky clearance that hit our skipper and somehow ballooned into the net.

Cue a hell of a weekend with me leading from the front. By coincidence, Dublin was our destination so, as the local lad, I led the way round the night venues in Temple Bar. It was a great lads' weekend in fancy dress and served a purpose for the team. Playing alongside each other on the football pitch is one thing, becoming good friends is another. When teammates share a good laugh, it honestly does bring you closer as a group.

If that went as planned, the rest of my Christmas certainly didn't. Mind you, there were a few jokes about me knowing what I was doing when I was sent off in the home match against Lincoln City and banned from the festive programme.

The incident came shortly after half time as I tried to keep dangerman Matt Green quiet. They played the ball forward and I knew Green, who had good pace, would try to get to it first and spin behind me. In my mind, I was timing my tackle to get there fractionally before him. Unfortunately, I mis-timed it and it looked horrible. No complaints about the red card, but it was completely unintentional.

Mike Flynn made a few cracks about me booking my Christmas holiday but, in truth, was disappointed with me. To ensure that I didn't feel rewarded, I was given extra running to do in training.

The rest of Christmas, however, was great. I spent it at Matty Dolan's house as his girlfriend, now fiancée, was away in Hartlepool. It was probably the first time in seven years that I had a proper Christmas. In previous years I had to be fit and ready if called upon. This time I could enjoy myself. League One and League Two footballers don't get anything like the same financial rewards as elite players but make the same personal sacrifices – and Christmas is high up the list.

The lads kept in touch with the play off places with a win, draw and a loss and played well enough to ensure that I was down the pecking order come FA Cup third round day.

Of all teams, we had drawn Leeds United for the second time that season. But this was at Rodney Parade rather than Elland Road and Leeds made nine changes. Only Gaetano Berardi and Kalvin Phillips, now an England international, retained their starting places from their last Championship match.

As underdogs, you look for any advantage and we genuinely felt we had a chance. A rocking atmosphere at Rodney Parade and the pitch favoured us. Also, their team selection hinted that Leeds thought they would win comfortably.

No way would we pick anything other than our strongest available side. Mike Flynn's team selection was always aimed at giving us the best possible chance. Rotation never entered his mind apart from the EFL Trophy. Ben White got the nod alongside Mickey Demetriou at the heart of our defence with me on the bench, kicking and heading every ball.

Although we went 1-0 down early on, we had chances throughout. Our big break came with about 15 minutes left when Frank Nouble's cross deflected first off Padraig Armond, then United's Conor Shaughnessy and nestled in the back of the net. That set up a cracking finale and when Armond had a late header saved, and substitute Paul Hayes fired just over, we were beginning to think of a second trip to Elland Road. Then fellow sub Shawn McCoulsky sent Rodney Parade wild with an 89th minute header to put us 2-1 in front. There was just time for me to come on in added time for man of the match Robbie Willmott. Not for the last time, Flynny trusted me as the man mountain to bolster our defence and close out a game.

Getting into the fourth round of the FA Cup was almost unchartered territory for Newport and it felt like we were putting the area on the map. This was the first time over the next few years when we got a reputation as giantkillers, particularly at Rodney Parade. We all sat at home listening to the draw but in close contact online to share our thoughts. The reaction when we were paired with Tottenham Hotspur was off the scale. A top Premier League side was on its way to Rodney Parade and they'd be as unfamiliar with what they found as Leeds United!

Again, I was on the bench. Gutted that I was missing out on such a big occasion and determined not to just be an occasional starter, I still shared the excitement of a tremendous occasion in front of the TV cameras.

Tottenham didn't make the same mistake as Leeds, naming a strong side led by Harry Kane and featuring Eric Dier, Kieran Trippier and Jan Vertonghen. We gave mighty Spurs a hell of a shock in the first half as we had chances and near misses, before Padraig Amond thrilled the vast majority of nearly 10,000 fans by nodding us in front after 38 minutes.

It took a full hour before Harry Kane and co came to the party. Then time seemed to stop. Mauricio Pochettino's side had several chances to equalise as we longed for the final whistle. We were only eight minutes from glory when Kane scrambled in the equaliser.

Disappointing as this was, the reception we got at the end,

along with praise from Pochettino and the media and a Wembley replay was very good consolation.

What happened before the return game is something we joke about now – but was no laughing matter for me at the time. I was almost certain that I'd be starting and very possibly marking England legend, Harry Kane. Nobody wants a colleague to get injured, but Ben White had gone down with a hamstring injury and I was next in line. When we trained, focusing on team shape, I was in the side and that's how it was as we travelled south on the Monday. Ben White was having a scan at Brighton, his parent club, as we prepared for the big challenge ahead.

Flynny was called to the front to take a phone call. That was when his mood and mine changed. I was playing cards with the rest of the lads when, with great glee, the manager said he'd just received the best possible news – Ben White was fit to play after all! He was laughing and, without a moment's thought, told me I was dropped! I couldn't believe it – in fact, I didn't! I thought he was joking as he wouldn't break bad news to me like that.

I still didn't believe it when Ben White joined us at the hotel. It was only when the manager called us together to confirm the side, I realised I really had been dropped. To make things worse, Flynny spent time going round other lads not in the starting line and still didn't speak with me. I was raging although, as I've said, we've long since seen the funny side.

The fans once again did Newport extra proud that night with an estimated 7,200 travelling to support us at the famous stadium on a Tuesday night. Spurs again named a very strong line up with Kane on the bench, offset by his partner in crime Son Heung Min and Llorente starting up front.

We were well beaten with Spurs scoring their two goals in the first half. But we left London with heads held high after performing very creditably and I had the consolation of getting 15 minutes after replacing Ben White. I'm not making excuses, but the sheer physical and mental effort of twice going toe-to-toe with a top side, not once but twice, did have an affect on us back in the league.

After edging into the play off places after a 2-1 home victory over Crawley, we were beaten at both Lincoln City and Colchester United between the two Spurs ties. On the Saturday after Wembley, the wheels well and truly came off at Mansfield Town where we were 4-0 down at half time. Again, I was the one the manager trusted to try to hold things together as I came on for Matt Dolan for the second half. It was a way back into the side even though that was scant consolation for a 5-0 thrashing.

The following week's home game against promotion chasing Notts County was now even more important. There wasn't as much riding as their previous visit, but we needed to stop the rot. In the circumstances, a 0-0 draw was a good result.

Although Paul Hayes helped himself to a hat trick in a rollercoaster 3-3 draw with Forest Green Rovers and we got ourselves back to winning ways at Yeovil, we never reached the same heights in the closing weeks of the season. Perhaps it was a cup hangover, who knows? As I've said, we treated all games the same way and had the right attitude, but had to settle for a very respectable mid-table finish.

One personal highlight of the run in was playing my part in holding promotion chasing Luton to another 1-1 draw at Rodney Parade. I had the tough task of marking the likes of James Collins and Danny Hylton, a formidable duo particularly at set pieces. There was plenty of good-natured banter during the game's quieter moments.

It was a difficult game against forwards who knew their business and put themselves about. I was pleased with my performance and it mattered not a jot that I still didn't get a handshake from Nathan Jones. Luton were promoted at the end of the season.

After my usual break in Dublin, there were a few changes to take in as I approached the following season. Domestic-wise the off-field partnership of Demetriou and O'Brien was broken up as his wife had just had a baby and they needed their own place. But I didn't go far – an apartment just across the road.

Team-wise we upped the quality with some of the players coming in. Joining us from Scunthorpe United was midfielder Andrew Crofts, who took over from Joss Labadie as team captain with me being captain off the field.

Although injury forced him to bide his time to make his debut, Crofts proved an inspiration skipper in every sense. The guy was a leader, a man among men and had the knack of saying just the right thing.

I recall him before a big night at Rodney Parade pulling us together and telling us that everyone had come to see us play – our friends and family included – and being out on that pitch was the perfect place to be. Fight for each other, kill for each other if necessary and have the back of every one of your teammates, he said. After that, I was ready to run through a brick wall for him.

Striker Jamille Matt came in from Blackpool and formed a strong partnership with Padraig Amond, bagging more than 40 goals between them in all competitions. Other newcomers included the talented former Bristol City duo of Antoine Semenyo, who represented Ghana at the World Cup in Qatar, and Tyreek Bakinson.

Disappointingly for me, a slight hamstring tear in one of the pre-season games put me out of contention for the League Two kick off. The early story was success on the field and chaos off it – the usual Newport way. One of the biggest problems was the accidental burning down of part of our training facility at Spytty, about 10 minutes' drive from Rodney Parade. Our stand-in kit man put the dryers on, left the building and it caught alight. Some of the kit and most of the building was burnt to a cinder. This caused disruption to our normal routine. We trained as usual but, instead of staying together to eat, we had to go here, there and everywhere for a short while.

Nevertheless, despite an opening day defeat at Mansfield Town, the lads racked up three wins and a draw to go into the trip to Port Vale in high spirits. That was an afternoon that never looked like going to plan until we got on the pitch. The lads had a laugh when waiting for our usual coach and being confronted with what looked like a school bus.

This was typical Newport and immediately caused problems. Wayne Hatswell arrived with our meals in his car only to find that there was no microwave on our dumbed down form of transport. Plan B then went to pot as Wayne's idea of stopping at motorway services to buy a microwave bit the dust because there were no plugs or sockets on the bus.

I sat on the bus with Matty Dolan as the lads sang *We're All Going on a Summer Holiday*, making light of our problems. Instead, we made an unscheduled stop at services near Stoke and had a pre-match meal with a difference. Forget the chicken and pasta or scrambled egg, we ordered 25 Katsu curries from Yo Noodle and sat on the bus tucking into our unexpected treat.

That went down well with nearly all of us, although Dan Butler asked to be substituted because he 'wanted a shit'. Told to carry on, he netted the winning goal a few minutes later in what, all things considered, was a remarkable 2-1 away victory.

I came on for the last 15 or 20 minutes to make my day complete. That was my first involvement of the season playing-wise and in a game that typified what we were all about. No matter how high the odds were stacked against us, we all got stuck in and fought for the cause.

That was a time when the Papa Johns (EFL Trophy) became my friend. Naturally I understand the reservations of some managers and players as games add to an already gruelling 46-game schedule in Leagues One and Two but, for me, they couldn't have come at a better time.

I needed match time to get fully ready for a return to the side and the EFL Trophy was where I got it. A 1-0 defeat at Swindon Town on a Tuesday night may not have been everyone's cup of tea, but I had looked forward to getting a full 90 minutes under my belt, so was well pleased with my evening's work.

A couple of weeks later, I was part of an experienced side that gave Chelsea's Under 21s a lesson at Rodney Parade. They had a team laced oozing potential including, Billy Gilmour, Conor Gallagher and full back Tariq Lamptey, who has since become a regular at high-flying Brighton. We knew exactly what to expect that night. They would play high quality passing football but how would they cope with our physicality and know how?

We introduced their youngsters to the game's dark arts and played our own style of football to run out convincing 3-0 victors. Jamille Matt helped himself to a double and Semenyo rubbed salt into young wounds at the death. It's not every day that you beat a Premier League club 3-0 and we enjoyed it! Not bad also from a team who had just been beaten 6-0 in our own backyard by Yeovil Town!

I'd like to explain exactly how that happened, but I'm struggling. Yes, we made many mistakes and, yes, Yeovil played very well and punished us to the full. At one stage, it seemed that every time they came forward, they created a good chance or scored. A terrible afternoon got even worse when Robbie Willmott was sent off. At least after I came on in the 84th minute, it was 0-0!

Damage was limited, not by my brief contribution, but the way it was handled by our management team. In many clubs, players would have been hammered all week after such a thrashing. Instead, Yeovil wasn't even mentioned until Wayne Hatswell fronted us up in the dressing room minutes before the following Saturday's match at Tranmere Rovers.

Not that the two of them were happy with the way we played – not at all. They were very, very disappointed. Yet they did all they could to keep our spirits up and put things in perspective. Our extra chores were all practical and useful rather than a punishment. Instead of our usual Monday morning training routine, we were on our hands and knees cleaning and clearing up our damaged building.

That was a job well done because it was a welcome boost to our morale to get it back in action. Afterwards we picked our lunch from the burger van with our failings at the weekend seemingly forgotten.

I applaud our management for this. We were a bunch of professionals and knew full well how badly we had played – the last thing that we needed was to have that same point hammered at us repeatedly. Very few footballers, if any, play poorly deliberately or lose matches without feeling hurt. And none of those played for Newport County during my years with the club.

Our rule of thumb was always the same after a loss – don't lose the next one! Wayne didn't spare any words and threw in a few expletives to tell us in that dressing room how poor we had been against Yeovil and that our task at Prenton Park was to win in any way possible.

Come 5pm, their tactics had been justified. Flynny again gave me a vote of confidence by restoring me to the back three, alongside Mickey Demetriou and new signing Fraser Franks. Together we did the job. Franks gave us the lead early on and we worked hard towards the end to protect a much-needed three points when the home side put us under real pressure.

That week highlighted that one game is only one game. Yeovil lost 3-0 at home to Swindon and we ended the weekend in third place, five points ahead of the team who humiliated us.

Unfortunately, my rollercoaster Newport career took another downturn, despite a 4-2 home win over Cambridge United. The first ball down the middle of our defence saw me suffer a reoccurrence of the hamstring injury from pre-season. So, just as I was beginning to get back into the side, I missed the next three games.

I was back in time for another of our strange away days at Bury. Heavy traffic made an already long journey into a five-hour marathon, with no way of stopping at our designated hotel for our pre-match meal. Instead, we ate on the bus and had our team meeting whilst completing an exhausting journey. When Flynny said afterwards it was a 'very, very good point', he was probably referring as much to our off-field problems as the challenge which the home side had presented on it.

One of the themes of my Newport story is our exploits against bigger clubs in cup ties. When facing very unlikely odds, we came up with the goods again and again. We enjoyed being written off and the pressure on teams expected to thrash us.

However, our best ever FA Cup campaign started with the boot very much on the other foot. I'd never even heard of our fourth qualifying round opponents. But I will always remember now that Metropolitan Police have a good football team after giving us a real fright.

It was lashing down with rain, the pitch wasn't great – and that's by our standards! – and the home side gave us a difficult welcome. This was their cup final with Newport County the giants. I sat on the bench cringing and biting my nails as the Police tore into us and could easily have been two or three up inside the opening 15 minutes.

I was waiting, half expecting disaster to happen, but instead we started to turn it around and Padraig Amond gave us the lead in the 41st minute after having an earlier effort disallowed. It was his partner in crime, Matt, who lashed in a crucial second three minutes after half time and, with the home side going down to ten men, a very difficult afternoon became much more comfortable.

I was back in the starting line up a few nights later as we

defeated Plymouth to go into the knockout stages of the Papa Johns. A full 90 minutes was a personal tonic and, yes, I was dreaming of Wembley. It may not have had the same prestige as the FA Cup, but I would have loved to have won it.

One downside from our good progress on all fronts was that our manager was beginning to get linked with other clubs. There was considerable speculation at this stage about Flynny being linked with Shrewsbury and we were pleased to hear him rubbish that after a 3-1 win over Northampton.

That could have been an even better evening for me after the two sides swapped early goals. Not a noted goalscorer – it hadn't happened since my special against Notts County – I thought that I'd broken the spell when meeting a first half free kick with a firm header. The ball was definitely on its way in at the far post when up popped Jamille Matt 'just to make sure'. Those were his words – he stole my goal! That's how strikers earn their living and, if anyone had to do it, I'd have settled for Jamille who is a terrific lad.

The second round of the FA Cup was a local derby. I'm talking tongue in cheek if anyone knows how far Newport is from Wrexham. It's a good three hours, further than some of our league trips.

We were, however, rivals. I wasn't aware of it but Wrexham's motivation for getting one over on us was about more than being a fellow Welsh side. One of their biggest disappointments during their 15-year exile from the EFL, which finally ended amid much publicity in 2023, came back in 2013 when Newport defeated them 2-0 in the play off final.

The atmosphere among the supporters at the Racecourse Ground was white hot. Warming up in front of our own very vocal visiting supporters, we were roundly booed by the Wrexham fans as we went back off the pitch. I was part of a three-man defence put under a lot of pressure and grateful for an incredible save by Joe Day. I'm not sure that even he knew how he did it. A volley came in from around the penalty spot and he threw out his right arm and somehow kept it out. Half time arrived with the scoreline still blank and the National League side still having most of the play and chances.

It was then that our kitman – this time our permanent one

Ian Turner – made an unfortunate contribution. Usually, the team goes into the dressing room and the manager takes a short while to compose himself before making comments. That's what happened here but, for some reason, the kitman decided this was his opportunity to say his piece.

He didn't hold back either, saying we 'needed to be f----ing better'. He wasn't wrong, but it wasn't his place to say so and we let him have it full barrels. Our general message was 'shut the f--- up' before Flynny and Wayne entered the room to give another version of Turner's talk. Again, we all laugh about that incident now. Anyway, we were a bit better in the second half but needed a great goal line clearance from Mickey Demetriou to book a replay.

As one door to Wembley stayed open, another shut as we were beaten on penalties at Cheltenham in the Papa Johns; and we somehow lost back in the league 2-1 at Swindon, despite playing with the strongest of winds at our backs and equalising early in the second half.

We needed to beat Wrexham to keep our FA Cup running going and regain our momentum. We always felt more confident in front of our home fans and had the incentive of a possible third round tie against Premier League Leicester City, who incredibly won the title in our 'great escape' season. That meant TV cameras and a guaranteed big pay day.

We were given a boost by the early dismissal of a Wrexham player and we took full advantage in the second half when we banged in four goals. This was the highlight of our pre-Christmas programme but there was no festive cheer.

A five-game run in which we took just one point tested Flynny's patience to the limit. I was in the side that had a chastening experience at Lincoln City when the Cowley brothers were leading a physically strong long ball side on course for the title.

We knew what to expect facing lads such as Jason Shackell, Michael Bostwick, John Akinde and Matt Rhead and weren't disappointed. When they won an early free kick 18 yards out, a siren went off in anticipation of an air raid and that set the pattern for numerous set pieces. We went 2-0 down inside 10 minutes and, despite two goals from Padraig Amond, our poor start proved decisive as we lost 3-2.

If being undone by 'ugly' football was bad enough, there was no consolation being well beaten by the 'beautiful' stuff. Visitors Forest Green were renowned for the style of their play and were a handful in the first half when they led 2-1. But that became a nightmare soon afterwards when Dan Butler was shown a red card. Chasing the game with a player short wasn't the best Christmas present as we ended up well beaten. I came on as an early second half substitute as it was thought that I couldn't play full back-to-back games.

True to form, we managed to dig out a 0-0 draw at home to Crawley in our next game, but our poor run was extended by two further away defeats with, unusually, Flynny beginning to lose his cool.

The trip to Stevenage was an important one for me personally as Dino Maamria, the man who had brought me to Newport, was their manager. I was motivated to produce my best performance, not only for the team but to show Dino that his confidence in me was justified. The game seemed to be turning in our favour when Kurtis Guthrie was shown a straight red card five minutes before half time for a two footed challenge on Fraser Franks. This was despite us already having failed to take several chances.

Padraig Amond, who had been banging in the goals, couldn't hit a barn door. Most of our opportunities fell his way and, for whatever reason, he just couldn't reproduce his usual form. Nevertheless, we were still confident at half time that, with 45 more minutes against ten men, we would make our advantage count.

Our pressure was mounting when Dino produced a masterstroke. Bringing on big striker Alex Revell on the hour gave us more to think about defensively when we wanted to push on and score goals. Revell was an experienced, worldly forward, all arms and elbows, who always reminded defenders that they were in a battle.

With us still unable to finish and beginning to settle for a point, Stevenage got a set piece in the 91st minute as we entered four minutes of added time. That's when the seemingly inevitable happened. The ball was crossed into our penalty area and Revell rose highest to head into the net. Stevenage one,

Newport County nil. Somehow, we lost when everything was in our favour.

As I've said, Flynny was very good at not getting too high or too low but couldn't contain his frustration. He rounded on our leading scorer by saying: "You are trying to get me the sack! Every chance you had, you managed to miss." Poor Padraig was beside himself. He was almost in tears as he replied: "Never in my life have I ever thrown a game of football."

It was the sort of incident that we can laugh about now but was serious and traumatic at the time. It was Flynny's way of saying we needed to get our act together very quickly or we would blow our promotion challenge. We'd slumped from a reasonably comfortable play off spot to mid-table inside a few weeks.

That meant we went into our third round FA Cup tie against Leicester in poor form. Disappointingly for me, I was left on the bench as Flynny decided to go with the side who had done the FA Cup business against Wrexham. Fair enough. This was the sort of occasion we thrived on – a full ground, winter weather and a difficult pitch. Not to mention TV cameras sniffing for a shock result.

Again, their team selection slightly opened the door for us. Claude Puel left out goalscoring talisman Jamie Vardy completely and put James Maddison on the bench. Nevertheless, there were five Premier League winners in their starting line-up.

The opening 10 minutes set the scene for what followed. Joe Day made a couple of good saves before we produced an outstanding moment to send Rodney Parade into ecstasy. It was a superb run and cross from Robbie Willmott and Jamille Matt rose above Leicester skipper, Wes Morgan, to net a perfectly placed header. That highlighted what an amazing sport this is. For several weeks, our strikers had been out of form and out of luck. Now, in a single moment, that was all forgotten.

Welsh international goalkeeper, Danny Ward, twice prevented us from doubling our lead. He did well to block a shot from Matty Dolan, then he smothered to deny Matt from a good cross by Padraig Amond. Almost inevitably there were plenty of Leicester chances, too, with Marc Albrighton nodding wide from a great position and Shinji Okazaki's effort brilliantly blocked by Mickey Demetriou.

The game was developing very similarly to the Spurs tie with Leicester throwing players forward in search of an equaliser and us defending for our lives and wondering with every minute that passed if our single goal was going to prove enough.

Like Spurs, Leicester broke our hearts with about eight minutes left. Day did well to keep out Iheanacho's header only for Ghezzal to lash in the rebound. At that stage the momentum was very much with them and we'd have probably snapped your hand off at the offer of a replay.

Yet football's a funny game and in the 89th minute Marc Albrighton, one of their experienced stars from their title win, handled in the penalty area under little pressure and the focus turned to Padraig Amond from 12 yards. I'm not sure what Flynny would have done to him had he missed but there was no chance of that as he sent Danny Ward the wrong way.

That's the sort of moment when commentators acclaim the 'winning goal' but we had to be on our guard. With five minutes of added time to negotiate, Flynny turned to me to come on and play in front of the back four to try to see the tie out. And that's what we did.

It was a funny feeling at the final whistle as the lads started their celebrations on the pitch. Mine was a little more muted as I literally only played for a few minutes and barely touched the ball. Nevertheless, I was delighted to have played even a small part in a famous Newport victory.

Having beaten Leicester, we were brought back down to earth with a 3-2 defeat to Crewe Alexandra, where I also came on off the bench, before finally getting our first league victory since November when Jamille Matt scored his 15th goal in all competitions to see off Exeter. That was a landmark day for me, too, as I was back in favour in a back three and helped the lads to a rare clean sheet.

That boosted us going to Championship side Middlesbrough in the fourth round of the FA Cup. We'd been drawn away at long last and against a very good side and were in almost unchartered territory. Nobody would have been surprised if we took a hiding.

Whilst it was all about the football for us, we were later told that the club would receive a guaranteed payment of £250,000 if we reached round five which is a considerable amount of money for us. It was great to realise we were not only creating great memories and history with our performances, but also helping to make the club more financially sustainable.

Flynny chose to go with a back four with me playing alongside Mickey Demetriou and we knew that we were in for a very tough challenge. Champions League winner, Jon Mikel Obi, was in the Boro line up having signed in midweek as we very nearly took the lead within 30 seconds when Padraig Amond went close. Our leading scorer also had a good opportunity ten minutes into the second half, yet, between those moments, Boro could easily have been in front themselves.

The breakthrough came around the hour mark through defender Daniel Ayala, and the tie then meandered towards a narrow Boro victory until we upped our game in the last ten minutes.

The story of our recovery was all about Matty Dolan, a Middlesbrough lad, who had been in the Boro academy and then released. He was desperate to show his home club what they were missing yet wasn't a certain starter in our side and had to bide his time that afternoon.

Flynny admitted afterwards that there was a bit of sentiment in his decision to throw Dolan into the fray when he replaced Mickey Demetriou in the 87th minute. He was our third substitution and our final throw of the dice.

Suddenly the chances started flowing for us. Antoine Semenyo went close twice and Jamille Matt forced a good save from Darren Randolph after turning and shooting six yards out. When such opportunities come and go, you do start to think it's not going to be your day. You hope and pray for just one more chance!

Then in the 94th minute it happened. The ball broke for the former Boro boy and he poked it into the back of the net. None of us could believe it – the perfect script. We knew the tide of the tie itself may have turned because Boro wouldn't enjoy coming to Rodney Parade.

Several reports suggested that we were lucky to stay in the FA Cup – I disagree. We had chances to be 2-1 or 3-1 up before we got our late equaliser. It's amazing how different a long journey feels when you've had a good result. The lads were buzzing on the bus, loving a late reprieve that felt like a victory.

Before the replay, though, came home truths. We could only manage a 0-0 draw at home to Port Vale and were smashed 3-0 at Grimsby. Our season was in the balance. We were doing brilliantly in the FA Cup but had to pick up the pieces in the league where we were a massive 10 points outside the play offs.

So, yet again, we needed to make light of recent poor form when Boro came into town. We had another incentive to upset the odds if we needed one. The draw had been made for round five and the winners were at home to mighty Manchester City, one of the best football teams on the planet. Couldn't be better.

One look, though, at the Boro line up and the size of the task was still huge. Up front they had Britt Assombalonga and Jonathan Hugill with big Rudy Gestede to come off the bench. There was no Jon Mikel Obi but good, good players in the likes of Daniel Ayala, George Friend, Adam Clayton and Aden Flint.

Of all our performances during my time at Newport, that may have been the best. Starting in the back three, it was my privilege to see us dominate Boro in every aspect of the game. Boro manager, Tony Pulis, was generous in his praise of our performance describing it as 'men against boys'.

The stats showed that we had 11 attempts on their goal in the first 45 minutes alone. How their goal survived an almighty goalmouth scramble in the opening 10 minutes I'll never know, and we could easily have had a spot kick when Adam Clayton handled. Padraig Amond went close three times without finding the net, but Flynny was looking on the bright side at half time. Rather than rueing missed opportunities, he told us that we were 45 minutes away from writing ourselves into the history books'.

It wasn't all plain sailing in our dressing room as goalkeeper, Joe Day, had even more on his mind than keeping Assombalonga and co at bay. He had missed the previous two games as his wife was heavily pregnant but insisted that he wanted to play. In the dressing room at half time, he was told that she was in labour and had been rushed to hospital. So, we needed to get the job done inside the 90 minutes so he could see her as fast as possible.

Rodney Parade was at its best with a large vociferous crowd and

Boro struggled to live with us despite Pulis changing his formation several times. We felt our big moment was coming – and it did.

Robbie Willmott was sensational that night and it was fitting that he came up with the all-important opening goal a couple of minutes after the break. I cleared the ball to the halfway line where Willmott won possession and went on a surging run. Seeing that he had little support, he left fly from more than 20 yards and goalkeeper Dimitrious Konstantopoulos got a hand to it but couldn't prevent it from going into the net.

This time there was no sitting back and defending our hard-earned lead. With Boro still struggling to create clear chances, we were very much on the front foot and got our deserved reward with a cracking goal straight from the training pitch in the 67th minute.

Padraig Amond was stood at the back post being marked by George Friend. As he made his pre-planned run round the back of the group of closely packed forwards and defenders, I moved to give him the space to meet Willmott's corner. If ever a plan worked perfectly that was it. Our fans were in dreamland. Hearing them sing 'Manchester City, we're coming for you' felt surreal. Oh Jesus, I thought, don't sing that too loud!

Back in the dressing room after the final whistle and we had won 2-0, it began to feel real for the first time. I'd been Newport skipper on a very big evening for the club and now we were set for something even bigger. Mickey Demetriou and I shared a big hug as we took in what we had just achieved.

Before the visit of City's superstars, we had two more home games to contend with and enjoyed mixed fortunes. Robbie Willmott scored the only goal against second placed Mansfield Town, but a late MK Dons winner meant that we went into the cup tie still eight points shy of the play offs.

As you can imagine, there was a lot of excitement in the build up to the City game with the fifth round being unheard of territory for us and the tie again attracting the live TV cameras. Then there was the prospect of facing world class players such as Sergio Aguero, Riyad Mahrez and Leroy Sane. We were used to going through our opponents after receiving reports of their playing style, now we were talking about facing up to lads who we enjoyed watching on *Match of the Day*.

We knew that they wouldn't change the way they played on our pitch. They would pass the ball from back to front for 90 minutes. Teams don't usually press City for fear of being played through and exposed, but we thought that this was our best chance.

On the Thursday when we focused on team shape, we had our first team playing against the fringe players. We pressed and they pretended to be Man City. You've probably guessed what happened. They played straight through us and scored! Not the confidence boost that we needed for when we faced them for real.

Wayne chatted to us about the game. In front of us was the prospect of creating history and producing one of the FA Cup shocks of all time. That meant a sense of seriousness. On the other hand, nobody in their right mind expected us to win, so we could go out there with no pressure and enjoy ourselves. In the dressing room, our talk was of how strong City would be. Pep Guardiola had a reputation for putting out near full strength sides in cup ties. Would he make an exception for lowly Newport?

I was first to find out! As Newport skipper, I walked out with Wayne to meet City's captain for the teamsheet handover. Oh f---- It was only David Silva, World Cup star and a fantastic footballer. Usually, I'd have shaken his hand and asked for his autograph!

Here I had to be very professional. I kept my feelings to myself and went through the formalities. We needed to be at the very top of our game or we could be very embarrassed. City had just beaten Chelsea 5-0 at Stamford Bridge when we were getting beat by MK Dons.

Look at their team: Ederson in goal, Danilo, Stones, Otamendi and Zinchenko as a back four, Foden and Fernandinho alongside Silva in midfield and Gabriel Jesus teaming up with Mahrez and Sane in attack.

Wow, that was strong! "Oh shit," said Wayne as he thought how to break the team news to the others. First, they wanted to know who the skipper was and gasped at the name of David Silva. Then Wayne read out the rest of the side one by one as the lads went silent. Robbie Willmott broke the tension by joking that City were probably going through the names on our teamsheet and shitting themselves.

Mike Flynn's team talk was short and sweet. He didn't have

to say much on an evening like this. If we weren't up for this, we never would be. Games like Manchester City don't come along very often, so go out, enjoy yourselves and create history!

The fans were there early with a virtually full stadium greeting us for the warm-up. They had come for the one-off chance to see Manchester City, but the whole occasion had me feeling very proud. As I led us out alongside Silva, the fans were going crazy.

We went into our huddle for a minute or so to get our thoughts together, then turned our gaze to see some very famous names in the opposition ranks. When the game got under way, City were passing the ball around like they were at Wembley. For 15 minutes we barely got a kick and had very little time to draw breath. If you haven't played against a side like that, you can't know how physically and mentally hard it is.

You must be continually on your guard as their movement is different class. With the ball glued to their feet, it takes it out of you physically trying to stay with them. Then it nearly happened. We should have taken the lead when a long throw from Mickey Demetriou was flicked on and Ederson did well to claw away a header from Tyreeg Bakinson. No disrespect to Tyreeg but had that ball fallen to one of our strikers, it would almost certainly have been a goal.

My task was to mark Brazilian striker, Gabriel Jesus, and later Riyad Mahrez – not easy. Jesus was probably the best forward that I ever came up against and I enjoyed the challenge. There's a huge gulf between League Two and a team chasing the quadruple, including the Champions League, but some things are always the same. And that was my experience with Jesus.

Towards the end of the first half, I came in from the side to tackle him as he tried to turn. I'd argue that it was a fair attempt to get the ball, but he disagreed. Rolling around on the floor with the referee deciding a free kick to City was sufficient punishment, he wasn't happy. He shouted his abuse in Portuguese – I didn't understand all of it but got the message. I picked out the words 'my leg break', meaning my tackle could have seriously injured him. As I came face to face with him again a few minutes later, he flung his elbow out and caught me. That's part and parcel of the game whatever level you are playing at and will never change.

We defended and defended as City relentlessly passed and

probed for a clear opening. A few minutes before the interval, I heard a shout from a well-meaning Newport fan urging us to get tighter and close the space. I turned and gave him a look as if to invite him to come and have a go against one of the best teams in the world.

The closest City came was a Sane shot against the bar and when, as the report read, I 'appeared' to block another effort from the same player with my arm. Fair play. I got away with one there, but nobody should begrudge us a slice of luck.

With VAR the penalty would have been given. In normal time with only one pair of eyes, the referee saw me throw myself at the ball and gave me the benefit of the doubt. Reaching half time at 0-0 against City was a real achievement. We became only the fourth team in Europe all season to prevent Pep's boys from scoring in the first half, ranking alongside the likes of European giants Bayern Munich.

Looking around the changing room, our lads were exhausted. Again, this is part of the game of football the fans don't see – yes, we'd kept City off the scoresheet, but they had caused us damage because it was unlikely that we could sustain that level of physical effort for a full 90 minutes. Nevertheless, our challenge was to tackle another massive 45 minutes, still with the prospect of causing the mother of upsets.

The turning point came only six minutes into the second half when Sane broke down the left-hand side, cut inside and shot towards the near post. The ball struck goalkeeper, Joe Day, in the face and looped over him and into the net. Going 1-0 down was a blow to our chances but didn't change our tactics. We were happy to stay in the game and you never know what might happen in the last few minutes.

The crucial second goal came as late as the 75th minute when Phil Foden, the brilliant young England international, danced through several challenges, including mine, and fired past Joe Day. Aside from Joss Labadie shooting wide following a long throw, we were confined to the ever more gruelling task of defending our goal as the minutes ticked by.

Then we had our golden moment two minutes from the end of normal time. How do you score a goal against the mighty Manchester City? The answer was a straight long ball down the middle that saw Padraig Amond in a foot race for possession with the City goalkeeper. He just managed to get his toe to it first and chipped it into the empty net to send our fans wild.

That was an amazing feeling – we had scored against Manchester City and given our supporters something tangible to take from a great occasion. That success probably went to our heads. In our naivety, we rushed to pick the ball out of the net and run back to the halfway line. We thought we could repeat the miracle and get back to 2-2.

That played a part in what happened next as Foden scored his second goal less than a minute afterwards and Mahrez added another. Everyone knew it and we knew it – 4-1 flattered Manchester City after our immense effort. We had gone toe-to-toe for nearly the whole 90 minutes and been just 2-1 down.

We did a lap of honour, soaking up the appreciation of our fans – a sentiment no doubt shared by most viewers on TV. We felt that we had given nearly the best possible account of ourselves on our big day. Without doubt, Manchester City were the best team that I ever faced on a football pitch. They have, of course, gone on to win many more trophies including the treble in 2022/23.

It's difficult to compare football sides from different eras, but my view is that the only side to match them was Barcelona when they outclassed Sir Alex Ferguson's Manchester United in the Champions League final at Wembley in 2011. That incredible Pep team, with Lionel Messi at his best and Luis Suarez and David Villa for company, takes some beating. We will never know how they would have fared against Pep's side of 2023.

That could have been the end of our season. Going through all that effort and emotion to raise ourselves for Manchester City might have made the rest of our League Two campaign a case of 'after the Lord Mayor's show' particularly as we looked marooned in mid table.

It was a great credit to the management and the players that what followed was the opposite of what happened 12 months previously.

Perhaps it was good that we were thrown back into the deep end just three nights later and, ironically after City, against the team at the bottom of the Football League, Notts County.

We expected a very hard game against a side now managed by Neal Ardley and fighting to prevent the unthinkable. A few days earlier they had turned over promotion seeking neighbours Mansfield Town.

I was in the side at Meadow Lane when we produced one of our best performances of the season to win away in the league for the first time since September. Jamille Matt bagged two goals as we led 3-1 before half time and Amond added a fourth shortly afterwards to seal a very important 4-1 win. Victory put us six points outside the play offs. Was a late surge possible after all?

Physical and mental tiredness may have caught up with us a few days later when, despite Joe Day saving an early penalty, we went down 2-0 at MK Dons. We had a reasonable sized squad but didn't have the luxury of being able to make many changes.

The next few weeks were very up and down with a couple of home wins and more disappointments on our travels but, from a personal point of view, I was delighted to be getting a regular run in the side. I must have been doing something right as six clean sheets in eight games kept us in with a shout of making those elusive play offs.

Finally, it came down to the last three games and the chance to play a couple of sides who could have mentally been on the beach.

Lincoln City had already clinched the title and were always a very physical side to play against. Atrocious conditions didn't help and it wasn't the easiest game on the eye. Whether Lincoln were most affected by having already achieved their mission, the conditions or our determination, I don't know. But we nicked a priceless 1-0 victory when Scot Bennett fired in off the bar and, with two games to play, we were only two points off the play offs with a match in hand.

Next game was at home in midweek to mid-table Oldham. Again, there was speculation that their minds might be elsewhere. Football, however, rarely works out as expected. We did our pre-match preparation knowing that The Latics normally lined up 4-4-2 and played long with an emphasis on the physical side. What we encountered was far different. Several youngsters were given a game and they began the evening knocking the ball around like Barcelona. This was the other side of the result not being of paramount importance to them – they played with confidence and freedom which can make a side even more difficult to beat. That was an evening though that will live in my memory for the rest of my life.

It had been almost two years since my famous goal against Notts County – but somehow during those 90 minutes I got two! More importantly, my goals enabled us to gain the three points after a challenging first 45 minutes.

The first came shortly after the restart after I chose to stay forward following a corner. Jamille Matt chested the ball down and screwed a shot towards goal for me to get on the end of it and divert it into the bottom corner. I remember wheeling away for my goal celebration and enjoying the good humour of the Newport fans singing 'Mark O'Brien, he scores when he wants!'

I'm still not quite sure how I managed a second and Robbie Willmott initially wasn't too impressed. The goal was awarded to him at first after he shot at goal and I deflected it in with my elbow. But he took it in his stride when eventually the powers-that-be ruled I was the scorer!

That put us in the play off zone for the first time in months with only one game left. Talk about timing! We were away at Morecambe whilst our nearest rivals Exeter were at Forest Green.

It was an agonising scenario with us one point ahead, but a much better goal difference. We had to approach the game as a must-win to put the issue beyond Exeter.

It's fair to say we didn't turn up – we weren't good at all. Former Newport academy graduate Aaron Collins put the Shrimpers in front as early as the 20th minute and, for almost all the afternoon, it looked like we were going to miss out on the play offs after all. We could easily have been two or three down at the interval but, with Exeter 0-0, we just had to go for it.

The second period wasn't much better and the clock was ticking. Finally, in the 87th minute after we had huffed and puffed, without particularly looking like scoring Jamille Matt popped up with the equaliser. Even after the final whistle, the tension wasn't over as we waited several minutes before being told Exeter that had also drawn.

Our vocal travelling fans celebrated what felt like a repeat of the 'great escape'. Through sheer spirit and determination, as well as ability, we'd again clawed back a sizeable points deficit in the last few games to achieve our goal in the most dramatic of fashions.

Mission accomplished, we had to prepare for a different challenge, an intriguing play off semi-final against Mansfield Town. Unlike us, they had gone into the last game desperate to avoid the play offs. They kicked off in an automatic promotion position at MK Dons needing a draw to pip the Milton Keynes side. Instead, they lost 1-0 and dropped into the play offs, something that we took as a bonus for us.

No matter how many times they said it was time to concentrate on the play offs, we knew they'd be hurting. In contrast, we had every reason to embrace the challenge. The play offs are officially cup ties and that appealed to us. Live TV coverage and the big build up was something we thrived on after doing so well in the FA Cup.

So, yes, we were confident despite finishing below Mansfield in the table. We were on a 10-game unbeaten run – could we extend that to a lucky 13 and gain promotion to League One?

I was skipper and leading Newport out in a play off semi-final was a great experience in front of another rocking crowd at Rodney Parade. My game, though, could easily have been all over inside the opening five minutes after a very controversial incident with their outstanding forward, Tyler Walker. The son of England defender Des, Walker had scored more than 20 goals for Mansfield on loan from Nottingham Forest, so I knew that I was in for a difficult time.

My problem came from a ball down the middle and seeing Walker about to make a run off my left shoulder. Pace was one of his strengths and, had he got beyond me, he would have been in a good position to open the scoring. I tried to pull him back with my arm and he cleverly locked his arm into mine. That meant as we started to run, we both fell to the ground. This looks for all the world as if the defender has deliberately up ended the striker. And, with me being the last defender, I was vulnerable to a red card.

I tried to influence the referee by my mock surprise that the free kick wasn't awarded our way but was very relieved when he only brought out a yellow. The Mansfield bench was furious and I knew that potentially we had got away with one. There was no let off a few minutes later though when Mansfield scored the first goal of the tie. They were known for their quick counter attacking and we were guilty of giving them an unexpected opportunity.

The goal came after we won a throw in near their corner flag. We had a well-rehearsed routine whereby Padraig Amond made a run but the ball was thrown inside instead, for Robbie Willmott to run into space. This time it went wrong with Mansfield nicking possession and racing up the pitch. The ball eventually reached CJ Hamilton, another of their pacey players, and he skipped through to find the roof of the net.

Ouch, that wasn't what we expected and it knocked the stuffing out of us for a few minutes. In the circumstances it wasn't such a bad thing for us that we went into half time just a goal down. This gave Flynny a chance to put the situation into perspective. We couldn't push too early and give Mansfield a chance to increase their lead, but realistically we had to get something out of the second half to give us a reasonable chance in the second leg.

Both sides sprung instantly out of the blocks and could have scored within the opening 60 seconds. Walker was denied by Mickey Demetriou's goalline clearance then Padraig Amond was denied by a great save from Conrad Logan. So, it went on with chances at both ends before we got a crucial break in the 83rd minute. Adebayo Azeez, who did a good job as substitute, got his toe to a ball over the top and went down under a challenge from goalkeeper Conrad Logan. The spot kick was disputed by Mansfield, but we thought the decision was right.

Up stepped Amond to take the kick as we held our collective breath. I'd have put my mortgage on him scoring from the spot if I had one, but Logan produced another tremendous save. This time, however, fortune was with us as the rebound fell conveniently for Amond to smash it into the net.

That changed the momentum of the tie. For the last seven minutes, plus added time, it was attack after attack from us and they were rocking. Our best chance fell to Joss Labadie who dragged his shot just wide as the frantic final minutes somehow failed to provide us with a winner. Some may have thought 1-1 made it odds-on Mansfield on their own pitch. Not us!

Their lads tried to get into our heads as we lined up before kick off at Field Mill, theatrically pointing at the grass to repeat the same old myth that we couldn't play on a proper pitch.

We stuffed those comments down their throats by playing great football in the opening 25 minutes. No exaggeration, we could have been 4-0 up and halfway to Wembley. Problem was we didn't score at all. Josh Sheehan went close twice; Padraig Amond had a chance and Robbie Willmott's shot was somehow blocked on the line by Ben Turner. In addition, the home bar was struck twice, once by Joss Labadie and then following a flick off Turner.

We were so much in control that, on the biggest home night of their season, Mansfield were booed off at half time. Naturally the thought was going through our minds, however, that this might not be our night. How many chances did we need to score?

Play was more even after the break with dangerman Tyler Walker and Danny Rose going close for them, but we had another memorable moment as Scot Bennett picked up possession in central midfield, ran forward and let fly from fully 35 yards. Last time I went back to Mansfield I swear the crossbar was still shaking. Honestly, though, that was the third time we had struck wood and still we were only on level terms.

And so it went on. Logan made another brilliant stop from Sheehan's volley and there was even an effort from me from the edge of the box that he kept out. As goalless games go this one was a thriller with Walker, for once, having a nightmare in front of goal. We were particularly relieved to see their leading scorer make a hash of a great chance with five minutes left.

Chances kept coming in added time despite both teams running on survival instinct and adrenaline after a punishing night. Both goalkeepers kept their sides in the game, although we would maintain that after 90 and 120 minutes we should have been on the coach celebrating rather than going through the trauma of penalty kicks.

When it comes to such a lottery, you are looking for any sort of advantage and I got one with a slice of skulduggery. As we tossed up for which end to take the kicks, I shouted tails. For some reason as the coin settled on heads, the referee pointed to me and said it was our choice. I knew that I had said tails but insisted otherwise to the clear annoyance of the Mansfield skipper. Perhaps we were beginning to win the psychological war after all!

We knew that we had five good penalty takers in our ranks and they all stepped up. Padraig Amond, Dan Butler, Reagan Poole and Mickey Demetriou put us 4-3 in front. Now it was Walker's turn. He had been Mansfield's penalty taker during the season but, over the 210 minutes of the tie, had either been denied by Joe Day or fluffed his lines. We were thrilled when Day again won their personal dual by saving the Forest man's penalty and giving us the chance to seal it.

Now it was Matty Dolan's turn. I had full confidence in him. When the ball hit the back of the net, it was mayhem. We raced to the touchline to celebrate in front of over 1100 away supporters. Then it was back on the bus, singing and dancing and on to a very late night back home in Newport where we thought nothing of dancing the night away in our tracksuits.

Whereas it had virtually been straight into the semi-final ties after the conclusion of the league season, we then had a near two-week break before the final at Wembley. This was done so that all three EFL play off finals could be held on the same May Bank Holiday weekend but made life more difficult for the players.

In effect it's a mini pre-season. The balance both mentally and physically had to be right. You must train hard to avoid losing sharpness, but even a small injury could mean missing the game of the season.

As a change of routine, we had a few days at Cardiff as we prepared for the tie. Overall, we were relaxed. Our whole story that season had been almost unbelievable, leading us to think that we were destined to be successful.

The two league games against opponents Tranmere Rovers offered few clues. We won by a single goal away from home before being held to a frustrating 0-0 draw on our own patch during our dramatic run in. I think that anybody who has gone through the play offs will agree it's very strange. Yes, there's the excitement of playing at Wembley, which for some is a once-in-a-lifetime privilege, but it's also a very short way of rounding off 10 months of very hard work. One slip or a piece of luck here or there and you are either in dreamland or feel that it has all been for nothing.

Among those who came to support me on such a special occasion were Dad, the Derby County scout Mark O'Brien and 'Spud' Murphy my former Cherry Orchard manager. It meant a lot to me that they all took the time and effort to be there for what was a very important game for me.

Sitting in our hotel room the evening before the tie, Mickey and I chatted and laughed. We couldn't wait for the talking to stop and the action to start – it was almost like waiting for Christmas in your youth.

What followed was a personal disaster, something that I will never forget and took months to come to terms with. Now when friends banter with me that I'm one of only two Irishmen – Manchester United's Kevin Moran in the FA Cup final being the other – to be sent off at the national stadium, I can share the joke. At the time, though, all I could do was cry.

I hated the thought of letting everyone down – the players, who had to battle through 30 minutes of extra time one man short, the fans, who saw us lose in heart-breaking fashion, and everyone associated with Newport County denied a perfect finish to our amazing season.

I can tell you, in all honesty that it wasn't all my fault. I admit however that I put myself in a position where the referee had to make a decision.

The game was predictably even with both sides making and missing chances. Looking back, it was probably a match too far for many of us. That was our 62nd game of the 2018/19 campaign, more than any other club in the first four tiers of English league, bar Chelsea who shortly afterwards played match number 63 against neighbours Arsenal in the Europa League final.

Nevertheless, we began well enough with Jamille Matt nodding wide in the opening minute and going close again shortly afterwards. My task after taming Tyler Walker was another massive one. James Norwood was the joint highest marksman in English football that season along with the great Sergio Aguero. One more goal would put him on top of the pile and potentially ruin our season.

It was his strike colleague Connor Jennings, however, who started the rot for me. I was sent off for two yellow cards and, if the second one was debatable, the first was plain wrong, in my view. Jennings received the ball from a throw in, turned and ran into me. The referee claimed that I had pushed him – which I hadn't – and showed me a yellow card. I told him that it was my first foul and he replied that my teammates had committed several, so he was booking me.

So, I saw yellow on a totting up process after not doing anything wrong? Even now, I can't see the logic of the referee's decision, but that's football. I probably wouldn't be writing about this now but for what happened in the 89th minute.

This was a similar incident to the one with Tyler Walker in the semi-final. I admit that I was culpable in that I instinctively panicked when I saw Norwood attempting to turn and saw the green space behind us. Again, I reached out with my arm to stop him and he locked arms with me before kicking at his own leg to send himself sprawling. You could call this cheating. I'm being generous in referring to it as clever forward play. They do it all the time and it is up to defenders to adjust.

Norwood stood over me, telling me I was f---ed. "You're going to be sent off," he said. Of course, he knew that I was on a tightrope from the first soft yellow card and he took advantage. I have many regrets and one was that I didn't compound the red card by hitting him. Now I'm glad I didn't.

I went straight into the tunnel where there was a TV showing the game and watched extra time sobbing with a towel draped round my head. Only a few minutes earlier I was convinced that we should have been given the chance to win the game and promotion. I was in the Tranmere penalty area when Jamille Matt got his toe to the ball and one of their centre backs brought him down. In fact, the ball came through to me and I smacked it against the post.

To our surprise, the referee waved away all our penalty appeals. Was it a spot kick? Yes, it was. Had there been VAR back in 2019, it would have been 100 per cent given. I'm not saying that the Tranmere defender deliberately kicked Matt, but he caught him and didn't kick the ball. That's a penalty!

Naturally after going a player down, the odds were on Tranmere. In my confused and sad state, I prayed that we could get to penalties. That would be 50-50. The lads did great, restricting Tranmere's chances to a minimum. But in the 119th minute disaster struck. I was watching, crestfallen from the tunnel, when Jake Caprice put in a very good cross and Jennings headed it into the back of the net. Life can be so cruel – and that moment, football-wise, was right up there.

Our season had gone up in smoke from the moment I got sent off – so I took the blame. I didn't have the heart to join the lads as they waved and took applause from our great fans. It took all my effort to go to the changing room where the lads and the boss did their best to reassure me that it wasn't my fault. But it was. That's how I thought.

When I saw Dad, I wanted to say sorry. Instead, he told me firmly and kindly how proud he was of me – I'd played well on a big occasion and done nothing wrong. His words genuinely meant an awful lot. They began the healing process for me. Afterwards I took to social media to apologise to Newport fans – and again they showed me what a great bunch they are. The response was very positive and sympathetic.

Losing in the play off final and being sent off seemed like the end of the world for me. It wasn't. There was much worse – and better, I'm pleased to say – to come!

CHAPTER SEVEN
MY FINAL WHISTLE

BEING sent off at Wembley isn't something that I will ever get over completely. To be brutally honest, I'm still bitter about the referee's decision. I still think about how things could have been so different. Had our stonewall penalty been awarded and scored, perhaps I would never have been left in that position.

Although Dad's words helped, I had never experienced disappointment on that scale in my football career. Losing is a part of the game that you don't like but come to accept. This was totally different because I took all the emotion from our defeat on my own pair of shoulders.

First thing to get through was the after-match party at a bar in London. Naturally, it was booked to celebrate victory and promotion to League One. Instead, it was a chance to drown our sorrows. As I sat there soaking up the disappointment, relatives of some of the lads came up to me and said that the referee's treatment of me had been terrible. That was good of them and I appreciated it. But, inside my head, it was all my fault.

Losing in the play offs means that the season ends instantly. That was good. The first thing we needed after Wembley was time off. Dublin was my perfect reset button. As I've written before, back home I was never Mark O'Brien, the footballer, but Mark O'Brien, the human being. That was helpful. I was able to get away from it all for a full four weeks, see family and friends and largely forget about football.

The other consequence of a playoff campaign is that pre-season comes around again very quickly. All too soon. I reported back for duty with all the other lads – a time of fun and smiles despite the thought of very hard physical work ahead. Yet I was much more reserved than usual. Seeing everyone again immediately brought back all of my negative feelings about Wembley.

There was an elephant in the room and Flynny dealt with it in his usual smart fashion. Instead of ignoring my long face, he confronted it – with humour. He said: "The reason we're still here in League Two is you, OB!" He meant it as banter and I accepted it as such. It was good man management to joke and move on, rather than pretend that it didn't exist.

Newport had rewarded my efforts with a new two-year contract just before the play offs. This meant, promoted or otherwise, they fancied me as part of the team. That vote of confidence was very timely and meant Flynny knew that I wouldn't take his comments the wrong way. Had anyone else have said it, I might not have been so forgiving.

My mind was now focused on what was coming next. Best way to make up for my failure was to do something positive. We had to put our Wembley woes behind us and get ourselves promoted, preferably automatically to avoid the potential lottery of the play offs. That was not going to be easy. I've already spoken about our FA Cup hangover – the problems we had two seasons previously after the euphoria of reaching round four. Now we had managed it so much better, using the high of playing Manchester City to drive us on to even better things in the league.

Play off hangovers do happen. Fans expect the team to pick up where they left off but, for some reason, often it doesn't happen. A good example is Huddersfield Town, narrowly beaten in the 2022 Championship play off final by Nottingham Forest, then relegation candidates for nearly the whole of the 2022/2023 season until they were rescued by Neil Warnock.

We had largely been together for three or four seasons and grown as a team. We were gutted not to get the outcome that we deserved but, boosted by a few new signings, were in good shape to go again. And so it proved.

The big kick off on Saturday, 3 August came with an unexpected twist of the knife for me. I went through all the physical work and pre-season games expecting to play and not thinking that I'd be suspended for one game because of the Wembley red card. I thought the play offs were separate from the league season and that I'd be ok. I found out I wasn't available about ten days before the home game against Mansfield Town.

The Stags were ironic opponents considering that we'd played them in two such close playoff games. Naturally they saw it as a chance for instant revenge. A 2-2 draw was a good measuring stick of where both sides were so soon after not quite getting promotion.

I didn't play the next league game at Cambridge either, but got in a very useful 90 minutes in a league cup tie at League One Gillingham. Again, we drew 2-2 but returned home victorious after winning on penalties. We had such good penalty takers at Newport, that I was never in too much danger of taking one. To be honest, I'd have put myself down after the goalkeeper. I didn't fancy them at all.

Next came another tussle with a side with high hopes of promotion, Plymouth Argyle; we were delighted to get over the line 1-0 against opponents who have since been promoted to the Championship, and to extend our lengthy unbeaten league run.

The Plymouth game saw me form a new partnership in central defence with new signing Kyle Howkins, who came on as substitute after Mickey Demetriou was unfortunate enough to break his leg. Talk about starting with a bang, it was Howkins who got our winning goal. More important longer term was how we slotted together as a partnership and helped us to another clean sheet. A good sign that we could make a dent on this division.

We were never going to score a whole heap of goals. We didn't set out to be ultra defensive, but were happy enough to be 0-0 going into the later stages of games because we had it in us to create opportunities and get a goal. With that in mind, our 0-0 draw at Walsall wasn't probably the best game in the world for the neutral, but one that I will always remember. Flynny said that it was my best performance yet in a Newport shirt and should be the level I always aimed for.

I felt good from the start. Bit of a football cliché, but how you begin a game is very important. I always wanted to win my first challenge, on the deck or in the air. That gave me confidence.

You think 'I've beaten him – and I can do so again' whereas getting done puts doubts in your mind. It's harder, too, if you mis-time your first header or tackle, to get into the right rhythm. It's almost a domino effect, everything tends to follow from putting down that initial marker. At Walsall, all my game was in top order – tackling, covering, heading, marking from corners, the lot. I'm not normally the type to pat himself on the back, but I knew I'd played well.

Another hard earned 1-0 win and a clean sheet against Crewe set us up nicely for our first high profile game of that season – a league cup tie at home to Premier League West Ham United. Our reputation as potential giantkillers encouraged the live TV cameras to come again. In addition, we seemed to be continually pulling big clubs out of the hat.

I have a permanent reminder of that night – the shirt of Pablo Zabaleta, the Argentinian international and Manchester City legend, who was in the Hammers' starting line-up. It surprises me to recall now that Manuel Pellegrini made ten changes to his starting line-up because there were some top, top players in that side, also including Ryan Cresswell, Issa Diop, Carlos Sanchez, Mikail Antonio, Pablo Fornals, Robert Snodgrass and Felipe Anderson. That's not to mention their most recent signing Jack Wilshire and current England star Declan Rice, who was on the bench.

When we saw their team, we knew that we were in for a big challenge – me more than most. One of my main tasks was to get to grips with Antonio, a big physical specimen and with a lot of pace. When a long ball was played over the top in the opening minutes and Antonio pulled up with a hamstring injury, I didn't feel too sorry. Result!

Like City, West Ham were undeterred by playing on our pitch. It was pass, pass, pass from the Premier League side but we certainly held our own in the first half. Fornals hit a post but, at the other end, Tristan Abrahams laid on a glorious chance for Padraig Amond who was denied by the goalkeeper's legs.

The turning point in the 44th minute could have been avoided. Kyle Howkins stalled on the ball allowing Wilshire to get a toe to it and go through one-on-one with Nick Townsend. Conceding just before half time isn't good at the best of times, but meant a mountain to climb against such high-quality opponents. We stuck at our task after the interval and had one or two opportunities. Yet it was mostly the Hammers coming forward and us dropping deeper to keep them at bay.

When we were beginning to push again for a possible equaliser, they caught us cold with a slick move involving Anderson and Fornals which finished us off. West Ham were a solid, solid side and it says much about how far we'd come that we left the pitch slightly disappointed. We rated our chance of beating them. Instead, we had to content ourselves with words of praise from a relieved Pellegrini and knowing that we'd played well.

I suffered a major blow three days later. Coming off in the first half at Forest Green Rovers. I felt my quad muscle tighten up and signalled to the bench to be replaced. It was mostly a precaution and probably caused by having followed two missed matches with a quick-fire run of games. In my absence, we kept our unbeaten league run intact with a 2-0 victory.

Strangely after facing the senior West Ham side, we hosted their under 21s in the EFL Trophy. I wasn't involved as I further rested my slight injury and Flynny again rang the changes. Somehow we managed to lose the tie 5-4 after being 4-1 up.

The fact that I was back in the side for the Port Vale game having made a full recovery showed that it was the right decision to come off against Forest Green Rovers. Still better we won 1-0, keeping yet another clean sheet and maintaining our fine start to the league season.

A quick look at the League Two table that September night shows that we were handsomely placed in second spot with our unbeaten league run now extended to 17. But, as many football folk will agree, it's when you think you have cracked it that things tend to go wrong. Nothing went as expected for us at Northampton Town and even our opponents were surprised at our tactics.

They started the game backing off, knowing that we liked to go long. This prompted Flynny to instruct us to pass out from the back and the home side responded by pressing us. The result wasn't good. And it wasn't my best day either. When a Northampton striker shot for goal, I ran back to the goalline and shaped to swipe it clear, only to connect with the outside of my foot and send it into the top corner of the net. I sat in the netting like a stranded fish wondering what I had just done.

The second, decisive goal in the second half wasn't too pretty either, being the result of a defensive mix up. Playing out wasn't our style and we weren't very good at it. My brief chat with opponents after the final whistle confirmed that Northampton were surprised by our change of tactics and took full advantage. To round off a bad day, Jamille Matt picked up two yellow cards in the closing minutes and we ended a pointless, disappointing 90 minutes with ten men.

At first, it didn't look like that setback was going to affect us too much as three games later we produced one of our best displays to beat highly placed Swindon Town 2-0 on their own pitch. Having started the game wary of the twin threat of Jerry Yates and Eoin Doyle, one of the best strike partnerships in League Two.

I made a goalscoring impact of my own seven minutes before half time. My header to put us in front was the fourth and the last of my professional EFL career. Yet it was the way that I did my day job that pleased me even more. I was putting the disappointment of Wembley behind me and coming into my own as a player.

Most things worked perfectly in Wiltshire. My goal came from a corner routine that we had worked on in training and, shortly after Flynny had introduced Padraig Amond from the bench, leading scorer turned provider, to enable Jamille Matt to clinch the three points with our second goal. That brilliant victory kept us in the top six.

My parents came to support me in a midweek clash with Carlisle and, although it wasn't the most spectacular of games, I played an important role in our 1-0 success. With the score at 0-0 and time running out, I was faced with a problem as a Carlisle player got free down the left and cut into our penalty area with another forward racing in for a possible tap in. I had to gamble – cut out the pass and make him shoot or face up to the striker. I chose the former and then flung myself full length to block the shot.

Normally that block was as good as a goal but, in this case, nothing could match our winner. George Nurse, on loan from Bristol City, came on in the 87th minute and let fly from around 35 yards in the last minute. I stood directly behind the flight of the ball and saw from the moment that he hit the ball it was destined for the back of the net.

The goal was spectacular and our celebration wasn't bad either. I was first to catch up with Nurse and wrestle him to the ground as several Newport players showed what it meant to all of us. The sound of the referee's whistle a couple of minutes later was music to our ears as we held on for another potentially vital victory.

I was enjoying life both on and off the field. Teammate Joss Labadie had come to live with me at the apartment and we were having a good laugh. There were nights out which weren't always predictable and meals in which certainly were. When Joss offered to cook, I knew the score. The menu consisted of fajitas, fajitas or, just for a change, fajitas! Fortunately, they were good. Once again, a man who started as a 'football friend' became a close personal friend and that could only be good for team spirit. Joking and fajitas aside, Joss was a great guy to go to for advice on subjects such as property and other matters.

Back on the pitch, it looked like the only way that the opposition was going to score was when I did it for them. The next one came against Scunthorpe when the ball was played down the line and I positioned myself at the near post. I went to shift my left leg to hack it clear and somehow it hit my shin and sneaked in at the near post. Luckily, we went on to win 2-1.

It was a tale of two spot kicks at Rodney Parade where we again showed resilience to grab a draw against Crawley Town. We were a goal down and heading for defeat when Tristan Abrahams came off the bench and netted a penalty.

Going into the match flying high in fifth place was no insurance against another unhappy trip to Colchester United. For some reason, we never seemed to play well there and it became an in joke. We called it our *Space Jam* moment because we were always cordially greeted at the ground by the same steward. Yet, after shaking hands, we seemed to lose all of our magical powers and became a sitting duck.

We briefly thought that the curse had been lifted when Abrahams put us in front inside five minutes, but it was soon business as usual. Our early goal sharpened Colchester's teeth as they tore into us with attack after attack. We were 2-1 down by half time and holding onto the ropes and it didn't get any better afterwards. The statistics told our sorry tale as Colchester totalled 18 attempts at our goal, including eight on target, whilst we never troubled their goalkeeper again after our early success. A final score of 3-1 barely did the Essex side justice.

Perhaps the curse extended to elsewhere as we began a very damaging run that reshaped our season. Our pride at ensuring that we didn't suffer back-to-back defeats was dented as visitors Salford grabbed a late winner as we were trying to see the game through.

Newport fans were almost expecting good times in the FA Cup, but this was one season when the cup stalled our league season. Round one in early November saw us make a long trip to a dangerous Grimsby Town who looked likely winners for most of the afternoon. Luke Waterfall gave them the lead before the Mariners absorbed a lot of pressure with time fast ticking away.

When Padraig Amond's header came back off the post, we may have been forgiven for thinking that it wasn't going to be our day, then yours truly did something different. I went up for a free kick in the 80th minute, got my toe to the ball first and was sent tumbling by one of their players. It hadn't happened before and it didn't happen afterwards, but my forward play enabled Amond to get us out of jail from the penalty spot. The former Mariner had returned to haunt his former club – and they hadn't seen the last of him yet.

That tilted the odds in our favour and gave me the chance of a perfect 27th birthday present come the midweek replay. I can't recall playing football on my birthday before and this was a good memory. Cup king Padraig Amond made it eight goals in his last seven FA Cup rounds by putting us ahead early in the second half, and flatmate Joss Labadie sealed the deal and made himself favourite to buy the drinks with a second in added time.

Winning was the main thing, but we knew how valuable these FA Cup runs were to the club's coffers. Even winning the competition barely touches the sides for the Premier Division sides but, for League Two clubs, rewards were massive for even winning a couple of rounds. It can be the difference between having spare cash to improve the squad and struggling to pay the bills.

A GAME OF TWO HEARTS

Our second round tie at Isthmian League North Maldon and Tiptree was again on TV and meant that we were playing for a guaranteed jackpot of £180,000. No pressure, lads. Problem was the cup matches – and we were also progressing well in the EFL Trophy – spread out our league fixtures and, when we did get back to basics, we couldn't buy a win or even a point.

Oldham Athletic were tough opponents at the best of times – not conceding many goals – and when we went a goal down to them, we feared the worst and couldn't do anything about it. Three tough, uncompromising opponents had produced three defeats and sent us plummeting down the table.

There was a downside to the trip to Maldon and any footballer on the wrong end of a giant killing will know how we felt. The home side were in the eighth tier, four divisions below us – so this was the equivalent of Premier League v National League. We were used to welcoming the cameras in anticipation of a shock, now the boot was firmly on the other foot. We'd have been the laughing stock of the EFL had we gone out to a team that many supporters had never heard of.

I looked fear, ridicule and abuse in the face that night – and it brought out the best in me. I will always remember waiting in the tunnel before going out onto the pitch – a stomach churning moment before any important game. In this case, the tunnel was a cage and there we stood alongside our Non-League opponents with a TV camera in our faces and home fans on either side hurling all manner of verbal abuse. That's a situation you either love or hate and it's swim or sink. For me, as I described at the City Ground a few years previously, such atmospheres brought out the best in me.

There were moments when the TV crew nearly got what they came for – goalkeeper Nick Townsend made one fine fingertip save among three vital interventions whilst another home effort went too close for comfort over our bar. Meanwhile we created and missed chances that we'd normally have swallowed.

There was another worrying moment for us midway through the second half when Kyle Howkins took a severe blow to his head during an aerial challenge and needed four minutes of treatment on the pitch before being taken to hospital. We needed to concentrate on getting a difficult job done, then check how Kyle was.

Thank goodness he was fine and thank goodness, too, for Padraig Amond. The scoreline was still 0-0 going into nerve jangling added time when our cup king got on the end of substitute George Nurse's cross and netted a thumping header. A 1-0 victory over a team so far below us wasn't a cause for mass celebration but worth its weight in gold in relief. Thanks to Padraig, we could take the victory and move on – get out of Malden as quickly as possible!

The live draw presented us with a visit to the original lion's den – Millwall – but not before our faltering league campaign suffered another setback. Bradford City's Valley Parade is always a very challenging place to go to at League Two level but, on this occasion, we were our own worst enemy. One fatal mistake ruined an otherwise good performance and we went home with nothing.

A bad back pass was seized upon in the second half by striker James Vaughan and, as he attempted to go round the goalkeeper, he was sent crashing to the floor. Nick Townsend got away with a yellow card, but a 1-0 defeat was our fourth league reverse on the bounce. If that wasn't painful enough, I came away with more scars. As I jumped for a header with Vaughan, he swung his elbow and caught me on my top lip which immediately swelled up and cut open. I was in a whole world of pain.

Don't mention that to Wayne Hatswell. His message to me on the sideline was: "Get back on, you big f...!" I know that sounds harsh, but you need to know the context. The assistant boss knew me inside out and which buttons to press. So, I took no offence, bit whatever I had left and got on with the game.

This game was played on Saturday, December 7, the night of our Christmas party. Talk about bad timing. The defeat was already enough to take the edge of what should have been a great night out in Newcastle but, as you can imagine, a lip three times as big as usual wasn't the ideal look. I felt like elephant man. The evening highlighted we weren't as tight a group as in previous seasons. Christmas parties can either heal wounds or make them worse – this was the latter. There was a divide among the players – mostly between older and younger lads – and a couple had personal differences with each other.

This was probably another factor in our decline that season.

When things aren't going well, it cranks up the pressure and this was maybe too much for some of the younger lads. No disrespect, but they maybe lacked the life experience to know how to react and went further into their shells. This isn't an easy sport. The first team game is so much more physical than under 21 level. That's why talented youngsters often go down a few grades and experience men's football for real.

Another factor that I think sometimes isolates young players is social media. Those of a slightly older generation have experienced both sides of this, including times when this wasn't such a big issue. In my view, lads can get locked into their own bubble through social media where they think they're communicating but they aren't. This is no substitute for talking things through for real.

The ways of the modern world are making people more individual at the expense of a team ethos which is what you need in football. This is a sport in which, however good you are, you can't succeed without the support and contribution of your teammates. Quiet rant over!

Things got even more ugly for me the following week against Stevenage. I was in the starting line-up after my head injury but had to give it up at half time after another knock. This one split my right eye open and left me beyond dizzy. Even Wayne couldn't have got me back onto the field this time! I'm not criticising the club but, despite it being a second head injury, it wasn't treated as a concussion issue.

They say things go in threes and that happened at Morecambe four days before Christmas. I started the game with stitches still intact and things started well with Joss Labadie edging us in front after 14 minutes. We had our chances to make the points safe in the first half, but the mood changed significantly after the home side brought on veteran striker Kevin Ellison and fellow forward Cole Stockton at half time.

Ellison was a unique character, later to play an important and positive influence in my life. On this occasion, he did what he did best on the field – lift the crowd and prove a total nuisance. A maverick by nature, he knew how to get on the nerves of a defender and didn't disappoint.

I was already in distress by the time Ellison appeared. A long ball down the middle caused the problem. Nick Townsend came out to clear, but their striker gave me a nudge and I collided with our goalkeeper. For the third week in succession, I hit my head and again the stitches were reopened. Immediately I didn't feel great, yet battled on until half time when I admitted that I was still shaky but agreed to give it five or ten more minutes.

Things got worse in the second half. As Morecambe started to create chances spurred on by the home crowd, I felt dizzy as they were awarded a free kick, went down on one knee and vomited on the pitch. I was struggling to see or move. I finally came off after Stockton equalised and before Ellison set up the winner. I was suffering from concussion – one of the clues is a feeling of heightened emotion. This was where the concussion protocols finally kicked in. I was given a scat test, being asked straightforward questions such as the months of the year. I answered all the questions confidently and thought I'd smashed it. Time to move on.

The protocols, however, insist that you must rehabilitate yourself gradually and I stuck to the rules. After a few days with no training, I was allowed to do some light cycling on the Friday, followed by more at the weekend and on the Monday. Then it was time to revisit the scat test – a light bulb moment. I did well second time around but realised how bad I'd been the week before. This was a lesson for me. As I'd been feeling fine between the games, I wasn't too worried about my head injuries. However, the tests showed that, irrespective of feeling physically fine, I really had been in a spot of bother.

It was no bad thing that I had a quiet, chilled out Christmas. Joss went back to his family, giving me time to rest and get mentally and physically fit. I missed three league games over the festive season in which we steadied the ship to an extent with a couple of draws before returning for our visit to the Lions' Den.

I knew something of what to expect through being on the bench for Derby County at Millwall and the atmosphere there is very hostile. As Nigel told us before that historic derby at Forest, you simply must not allow the home side to score early and encourage the home crowd even more. So what happened?

Man mountain Matt Smith was a handful for any defender, League Two or higher. A few years earlier he had scored twice for Oldham to help cause an almighty cup shock against Liverpool and it was one of my jobs to stop him. Yet, after just seven minutes, a corner came flying into our penalty area and there was Smith, all 6'13" or so of him, to poke the ball into the back of the net.

That made our big task much harder, but we stuck at it. Padraig Amond was in hot pursuit of legendary Stan Mortenson's FA Cup record of scoring in 12 successive ties. He so nearly made it nine out of nine from a rebound after Jamille Matt was denied – but that was as good as it got.

We created chances, particularly in the half hour after the interval, but it wasn't to be. It was my foul that led to the home side adding a second from the penalty spot and the tie finished 3-0 – a conclusive enough looking scoreline, although we were far from disgraced by our performance.

It was getting to the stage where we needed a win – any win – to get us back on track. And again the EFL Trophy came to our rescue. We'd already had a couple of memorable nights in the competition that season – losing the nine goal thriller to West Ham United Under 21s and winning 7-4 at Cheltenham where defences weren't on top. The 3-0 home victory over MK Dons in the knockout stages wasn't as dramatic by comparison. But we didn't care. I played the full 90 minutes and got that winning feeling again and that helped us to pull things round for a while.

The story of the next few weeks, both personally and for the world, is that you never know what's around the corner.

Things seemed to be falling back into place. I was over the head injury, back into the team and playing well – and we were winning again. My focus was on enjoying life and trying to lead us into another tilt at the play offs. We'd come from near oblivion to keep our Football League status, surprised everyone by scrambling into the play offs the previous season, so why couldn't we do it all over again? Sure, we were a few points adrift in mid-table, but there was plenty of football still to play – or so we thought – and we had experience of how hard it was for other teams to stop us when we got ourselves on a roll.

A 2-1 victory at Scunthorpe's Glanford Park was an excellent result and we followed that up seven days later by disposing of Swindon Town 2-0 at Rodney Parade. That put us eight

I scored a last-minute winner against Notts County on 6 May 2017. When the ball hit the back of the net, I just ran. We had achieved the 'Great Escape'.

My red card against Lincoln on 23 December 2017 looked horrible, but it was unintentional.

It was an honour to play at Wembley in February 2018, although we lost 2-0 to Spurs.

We shocked everyone when we beat Leicester City 2-1 in the FA Cup in January 2019.

With Michael Flynn. A legend who put the 'Newport' back into Newport.

We faced Middlesbrough in the fourth round of the FA Cup.

Goals from Robbie Willmott and Padraig Amond gave us a 2-0 win against Boro.

Leading out Newport for our FA Cup tie against Manchester City.

Gabriel Jesus was probably the best forward I ever came up against.
I enjoyed the challenge, although it doesn't look like he did!

I scored against Oldham in April 2019 to secure three vital points.

Play-offs here we come. Celebrating with David Pipe.

Celebrating with the Newport fans. They have always been great towards me.

Leading Newport out at Wembley in 2019 was a very proud moment.

Lining up with my Newport teammates before the Play-Off Final against Tranmere in May 2019. Sadly, we lost 1-0 after extra time.

I was sent off just a few minutes after we should have had a penalty.

With Tom Gittoes (physio) and Lewis Binns (sports science).

I always hated pre-season running!

Leading out Newport alongside West Ham's Pablo Zabaleta in August 2019.

Joss Labadie and I often doubled up on opponents. Here we are winning the ball from Millwall's Alex Pearce in the FA Cup in January 2020.

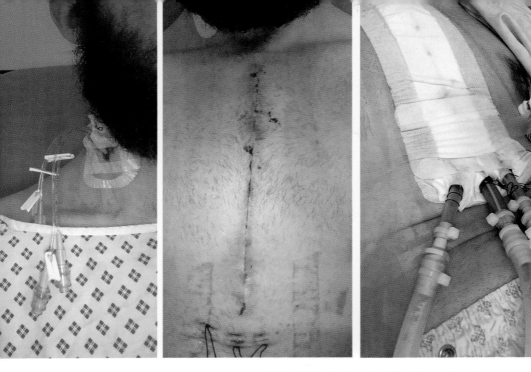

I had my second open heart surgery on 2 July 2020 during the Covid pandemic.
Sadly, it meant that my football career was over. I was still only 27.

Matty Dolan has helped me with everything and become
family. My fellow DJ.

I enjoy sharing my story
to help and inspire others.

I love my new role as co-commentator
on BBC Radio Wales.

It's good to give back and I enjoy helping
the British Heart Foundation.

Kevin Hendrick has helped me get back
into shape since my retirement.

Although I can no longer play, my role as
club ambassador means I am still very much
involved at Newport County.

points off the play offs but with two useful games in hand. We travelled to Leyton Orient next with confidence and I swear that I wouldn't have believed anyone who told me that would be my final professional match.

Looking back, it was an odd day even before kick off. My mate Joss got on the bus at Droitwich and told us that he wasn't feeling right. He was due to be part of the starting line up in Essex but was suffering from pains in his chest – a tough subject for me and one that was about to get much more so. Joss was taken out of the team and sent to hospital for tests where everything came back fine. Whether it was indigestion or a panic attack, who knows but there was nothing wrong with his heart.

Ryan Inniss also pulled out with a calf problem, so it wasn't the best of preparations all round. That was also a day when Orient renamed one of their stands after former manager Justin Edinburgh, who had died at the far-too-young age of 49, following a cardiac arrest.

Talk about a poignant and ironic moment considering what was going to happen shortly down the line. Edinburgh, the former Spurs defender and genuine nice guy, was also a legend in Newport circles. He'd been appointed with the club second bottom of the Conference and heading again into potential oblivion and guided us back into the Football League with a famous 2-0 playoff victory over Welsh rivals Wrexham at Wembley. The game itself wasn't that memorable and was at least accident-free from our point of view until the 81st minute. That's when the wheels came off big time.

Ryan Haynes scored an own goal to give the home side a 1-0 lead. That led me to take an ill-fated executive decision. Unlike against Notts, I didn't wait for the manager give me the green light to go forward, I just did it. I knew I was in for an earful because with us pushing forward in search of an equaliser, they made it 2-0.

I was even more desperate to make a difference and, after Padraig Amond launched an attack, I ran in behind the Orient defence and stretched out my right leg to try to get a toe to it. That's when their centre back came in and caught my leg and I was clattered by a couple of players. My right knee blew up immediately where I'd done my ACL in the past and my elbow

129

was also very sore. I was in a lot of pain and ended that afternoon with my arm in a sling and knee in a brace – a bad, bad place to be.

When we got home to Newport at about 9pm, my girlfriend didn't like the look of me either. She took me to accident and emergency where it was diagnosed that I'd broken a bone in my elbow. With the knee problem on top, I knew that I was going to be out of the game for some time – as it happened, it would be for life!

CHAPTER EIGHT
COVID, RETIREMENT AND HEART SURGERY TWO

By MICHAEL FLYNN, former Newport manager

THERE is one thing that I thank Covid for. But for that and his injury, Mark could have died on the football pitch – and I honestly don't know how I could have coped with that.

I knew about Mark's heart surgery at Derby, but his heart condition was mostly in the back of my mind because he played it down and we had regular checks at Newport.

Taking that phone call telling me that he was retiring and needing more heart surgery was horrendous. I thought he was going to tell me one of his awful jokes or update me on his injury. I truly shed tears when he told me the news.

Football then was the last thing on my mind. Mark's health in later life was all that mattered.

His is both an horrendous story and a great one. He went through really tough, scary times and it was important that he had good friends at the club, including Matty Dolan and Mickey Demetriou.

Happily, he has changed his life and that is very inspirational. I've heard about Mark's talks and the things that he has done on social media and his story goes beyond football – for people in all walks of life suffer from heart conditions.

When I was manager at Walsall last season, Mark and David Pipe looked after the kit when Newport visited and were the only people all season who swept clean the away dressing room – and I told that to the Newport manager.

I'm delighted that he's still at the club as he has so much to give, not least on issues such as mental health and anxiety because of what he has experienced.

I have got so much time for Mark and his close-knit family that I first got to know when looking after his brother James at Bradford City.

I wish him two more things: to improve his jokes and to find a lovely woman to settle down with!

*****

TALK about a shitstorm! Everything hit me at the same time and very nearly ended my life, let alone my professional football career.

Being badly injured and knowing that I could face another long road to recovery was difficult enough. Particularly as I'd suffered so many setbacks over the years which played a part in me moving clubs and not being able to develop my career as I wished.

This had happened when I was almost at the height of my powers. At a club I loved, I was playing regularly and well and my life was in good shape off the field. I was looking forward to the best part of my career when again it was all snatched away from me.

As it was during the time of the Covid 19 pandemic it made things much, much worse. Looking back, it affected me in a whole host of ways, contributed to the anxiety that virtually crippled me and certainly slowed down my recovery.

At first, like most of the rest of the world, we didn't know what to make of it. The season had moved on another ten games post Orient and our longed for run towards the play offs hadn't materialised. Results had been indifferent, and we were marooned in 15th place. I was still in the early stages of my rehabilitation, still not knowing when I'd be back on the field.

Now there was talk about a mystery virus sweeping the world. You couldn't get away from it. Whenever you switched on the TV or other media, it was there, but nobody knew what to make of it.

Footballers are renowned for living in their own bubble. It's been said, probably rightly, that anything could be happening in the world, but footballers blank it all out and focus on trying to win three points on a Saturday. That's how it was for a short time. But then the EFL and the Premier League called a halt. We were told that all football was suspended for three weeks.

The club closed and there was no official training. Yet we had to keep ourselves fit for when play resumed. This was like a pre-season when nobody knew when the new one was going to start. Very disorientating and confusing – but it was much the same for everyone.

We were told to stay at home and not get together as a team. Matty Dolan though was part of my bubble and we did our best to work and play without breaking the rules. We went out on what Matty now calls our 'magical cycle tour' which he remembers more clearly than I do. It started innocently enough with a cycle ride. We both had bikes and were quite keen cyclists, so it made sense to have a ride out – good for morale and fitness.

We rode for about 25 minutes to a place called The Sea Wall. It was a nice, secluded place and obviously, in the circumstances, we took our own refreshments. Both of us carried school bags – mine with four cans of Guinness, Matty's with four cans of cider. So, we had a quiet drink and a laugh until beginning to feel a little merry. Then Matty said he needed to get back home in reasonable time because of his girlfriend. No problem. It wasn't that long a ride to his house with virtually nothing on the road.

Nothing was as simple as that, however. For some reason, Matty decided to show me a party trick. It was something that he'd seen the top cyclists do when one would push the other over the line. It worked for them, so why wouldn't it work for us? He turned his bike towards me and went to push me, the handlebars turned and we were both sent flying, me into a layby.

Never mind. Not much harm done. We dusted ourselves down, got back on our bikes and cycled to Matty's house. There we were in his back garden enjoying the unseasonably good March weather when in came Matty's girlfriend. She offered us both some red wine and neither of us were in a mood to refuse.

It was a good day; we were both quite merry – ok pissed – and I remember having a fun game of hide and seek with Matty's young daughter. Suddenly it was 7pm and I made a silly decision. I got it in my head I had to go home. Matty played Mr

Sensible and said there was no problem putting my head down at his place and going back in the morning after I'd slept it off. But it didn't matter what he said, I wanted to go home.

I got on my bike, not once, not twice, but three times, and each time landed on my backside. Even that wasn't enough to stop me. I straightened out my handlebars and off I went. It was only about 10 minutes from home, the streets were deserted and I knew the way very well. Nevertheless, I somehow found myself in a side road with Matty in front of me. "What are you doing here?" I asked. "Didn't you realise?" he answered. "I've been following you all the way." I hadn't!

Matty made sure that I got to my front door and moved on as I prepared to climb the two flights of steps to my apartment. That I duly did and thought I'd done a good job. Next thing I knew I woke up at 4am and couldn't remember anything about my journey home. I spoke with Matty in the morning and he explained that I'd cycled, but I still couldn't piece it together.

He suggested meeting up for a beer, so I grabbed my bike and started walking down the stairs. I was spotted by the cleaner who pointed to the walls – tyre marks on every one! I couldn't deny my guilt, standing there with my bike on my arm. I was embarrassed, we laughed and I went on my way.

What happened next was no laughing matter. It was around the middle of March when I went out for a long walk in the park with my girlfriend. When we got home, I sat on the sofa and felt a big thump in my chest. I didn't know what it was and felt breathless.

When I went to bed, I lay on my left side and felt something similar. I texted the club doctor, Daniel Vaughan, to whom I'd honestly say I probably owe my life. At first, he tried to reassure me. I'd had a heart scan only five months previously and all had been ok. It was probably an ectopic beat, a cough was normally enough to put it back in rhythm, he added.

Things started to unravel a couple of weeks later. I felt really bad after going out on my daily cycle with Matty. I was a professional athlete, but seriously exhausted like an old man.

It was worrying, too, when my girlfriend and I did some exercises in the apartment and I had to stop because I wasn't feeling well enough to continue. This was time to consult our doctor again and tell him that I was feeling more and more exhausted. He said he would get me a scan as soon as he could although this was difficult because of the Covid problems.

I was feeling very mixed at this time. Naturally I was hoping they wouldn't find anything; on the other hand, I had this gut feeling something wasn't right. I had the scan and my girlfriend was waiting outside the hospital doctor's office when he told me the results.

"It's your heart valve," he said. "It's leaking – and it's leaking quite badly." I felt numb. But I knew exactly what to do. "I am going to have to retire from football," I said.

At first, he tried to reason with me, explaining that there was a procedure they could follow that might be able to get me back playing. But I knew that wasn't right for me. "When I was 16 years old and had my first open heart surgery, I said I would retire when it happened again. Nobody knew if it would be one year or 10 years, but that would be it. I need to concentrate on my health now," I said.

Sitting in my girlfriend's car after the devastating news, I cried. "Everything is going to be ok," she said, trying to help. I couldn't take anything in. We were in the middle of a pandemic and I was facing open heart surgery. Also, I'd lost the only job I ever had, one that had sustained me through the last 11 or 12 years.

How could I even begin to come to terms with all that happening at once? I don't naturally respond well to change – now everything that I thought I was in control of was crashing down on me. Or so it seemed.

Important people needed to know – and in the right order. I phoned Mum. Thank goodness she has the coolest of heads; if anything panics her, she never lets on. She took in the gravity of the situation straightaway, booking the next flight over from Dublin.

Next up was Michael Flynn. Not an easy call to make for several reasons. He had done so much for me. Alongside Nigel Clough at Derby, he was one of the main men in football who believed in me and gave me an opportunity. I was so proud to be his captain.

"Alright, mate, what's going on?" he asked, no doubt thinking the call was an update about my injury. "Gaffer, I'm going to have to retire," I answered. Cue a short, poignant silence on the other end of the phone before he said: "f--- off."

Then I told him my predicament. Quitting football was the last thing I wanted but, with potentially life-saving surgery imminent, my time had come. "No problem," he replied. Phew that was a big one out of the way and I was grateful for his understanding.

Next came the fans. And I've got to say this part surprised me and gave me a timely boost. I was a League Two footballer, many in the sport itself, let alone the outside world, would struggle to place me. I didn't think my announcement would merit much attention. I just needed to let people know who had supported me over the years.

I'm no big social media man, but I sent out the news on Twitter and Instagram and immediately people started messaging me. The club's physio and my former managers Stuart McCall, Nigel Clough and Nathan Jones (thank you, that was much appreciated) were among the early wishers. I switched on Sky Sports and my news was there, same with the BBC. I couldn't believe it. I hadn't really fulfilled my career (I feel differently now), so for people to show that they were thinking about me was wonderful.

I also had messages from teammates from Derby, Motherwell and Luton and opponents who caused me nothing but trouble on the pitch, such as Eoin Doyle and that man Kevin Ellison. It was very helpful to realise that, whatever I had or hadn't done on the football field, I would be remembered. In addition, ITV Wales interviewed me on my heart surgery and career to further spread awareness of what was happening.

I knew something of what lay ahead from my surgery at 16. The process, at least, was familiar. Yet other things were different. First time around, I had no symptoms to go with my diagnosis. Now I felt tired, breathless and dizzy. This made me feel more worried.

When I went back to Leicester's Glenfield Hospital, the scene of that first operation, I was a physical and nervous wreck. For the first time I was suffering from anxiety that was off the scale. I knew what it was like to be sick with nerves before a football match – that happened hundreds of times. But that was part of the excitement building up to something that I enjoyed. This was nothing of the kind. I wasn't eating properly, looked and felt ill and had no idea what the future held.

In the middle of June, I had an appointment at the hospital. They clearly felt the same way because they admitted me straightaway. Sounds strange to say it, but I was happy with that. It was an indication that my operation was going to happen sooner than later. I felt like my life was on a clock and time was running out fast.

Hospital was the only place where I felt safe. Glenfield is a specialist heart hospital. I'd been there before and knew that I was in the right place. I'd have struggled being at home for a couple of weeks waiting for the operation.

To make my situation harder, Covid meant visitors weren't allowed, so I kept in touch with loved ones by phone. There was also the added anxiety of 'what if?' – at one stage I was in a ward with Covid patients and worried about getting the disease in my very vulnerable state.

I pressed the alarm and the night doctor came to see me. I was feeling very sick, had chest pains and started to vomit. He gave me an echocardiogram as my heart rate and blood pressure were high. He thought that I might have an infection. That was seriously bad news as it could delay my operation when time was of the essence. I was moved into a main ward so that they could keep a close eye on me. They were treating this very seriously.

I wasn't sleeping well and felt alone. My sleep problem was partly because I was scared I might not wake up. With no visitors allowed, I was going through this entirely on my own. At least when I was 16, I had my family. This meant things I might have been spared were being given to me directly by the doctors. All this added to my anxiety and confusion as testing continued.

On the Tuesday I was given a provisional date for my operation – two days later, Thursday, July 2. This depended on there being no infection. Knowing that my heart valve was hanging by a thread, I was very emotional and burst into tears. I was praying that I didn't have an infection because I didn't feel I had much time left.

On the Wednesday the doctor gave me good news – no

infection! I burst into tears and shook his hand. Never thought I'd be so grateful for news that I was definitely going to have open heart surgery!

It's important here to mention how others were suffering. Whilst I was in hospital not knowing if I was going to live or die, those closest to me were also going through it. This was probably worse because they had to rely on me keeping them informed. I would like to say this: I am so grateful that during this time Mum had company. My girlfriend was brilliant with her, taking her wherever she wanted to go and generally offering support.

On the night before surgery, I was given the consent form. This was another worry that I hadn't faced as a teenager. I was confronted with the pros and cons of the procedure all on my own. There were no 'pros' of saying no – I would die! Going ahead, there was a 92 per cent chance of success. The remaining eight per cent included death. In effect, I signed my life away. This brought home the enormity of what was happening.

The operation was scheduled for about 10am on the Thursday. I was woken up for the usual pre-op procedures, such as cleaning, shaving and being given medication to make me drowsy. The extraordinary thing is that, whilst I was in the operating theatre, Mum and my girlfriend were outside. Rules were rules, but Mum demanded she be allowed into the building and a nurse agreed. She told me she'd given her word she'd be there when her son was going through open heart surgery and nothing was going to stop her. She really is amazing.

For some reason, Covid meant that I wasn't put asleep in the side room. Instead, I was wheeled into the operating theatre where I saw about 25 doctors standing round me. There I was given the anaesthetic and told that the next thing I knew the operation would be all over.

The operation lasted seven hours and I woke up in intensive care. My eyes were still shut and a nurse offered me water. It was the best water I have ever tasted in my life. I gulped down some orange juice and was sick. Better stick with the water. The nurse asked if I'd like to speak with my family. When Mum asked how I was, I answered "alive". I was "in recovery now" and Mum and my girlfriend need not worry. I was in intensive care for another day before being taken back to the ward.

All I wanted to do was rest, but a nurse told me that it was time to exercise – it was essential to get my heart working again as soon as possible. I still had all the tubes from the operation attached and walked with a hunch. She told me to try to get my head up and walk as normally as possible. Ten steps were the equivalent of climbing a mountain. I was so tired.

It was difficult to sleep with those tubes, but the walking was stepped up every day. I was on a ward with patients about three times my age but felt more like one of them than a professional athlete. Four days on, it was time to take the tubes out. I remembered this from my experience at 16. Yes, it was great to get rid of them, but the procedure wasn't nice. I felt each piece of long chord as they were taken out. Horrible!

They had also inserted a catheter, so that had to go too. I was numb and it was the weirdest feeling without being in pain. But, minus all the medical equipment, I felt more human. More than that, I was told that I was doing well and likely to be discharged within a few days.

My walking was getting longer each day – ten minutes, or two five-minute stints – and I was offered an exercise bike. But there were signs that I was still weak. I weighed 83kg when I went into hospital, now I was down to 70 or 71. I wasn't eating much and still didn't want to.

The discharge people came and spoke to me about my tablets. Then I took a turn for the worse. I buzzed the night nurse to say that I was feeling sick. My temperature was up to 39C, which is really high. I was breaking out in sweats and my heart rate was up.

When the doctors came round next day, I wasn't in good shape and they started checking for an infection. A scan revealed a dark spot above my heart – a possible clue. I'd been on a high after the relief of going through the operation. But the first sign of a setback rocked my confidence and made me more scared. Amid more scans, I was suffering from the fear of the unknown.

I was put on a drip line connecting with my heart and next morning the doctors spoke about still checking for an infection and possibly having to operate again. I was feeling desperate. This was the last news that I wanted to hear. I honestly felt that my body was too weak to take another procedure. Again, I was fearful that I might die.

What I needed most at this stage was reassurance that I would be ok. More important than the latest report on my condition was knowing that I would come through this. But nobody was giving me that reassurance.

Martha was one of the nurses who treated me. When she went off for a week's holiday, she expected I'd be gone when she returned. "What are you still doing here?" she asked. One look at me though and she knew things weren't right. I was wasting away and ill. I told her how I felt and she put me in a wheelchair and wheeled me outside for a chat.

I told Martha that the doctors coming round each day with their bleak prognosis was doing me no good at all. She gave me a promise. She would tell the doctors to stay away and get the surgeon to speak with me. That sounded good.

And that's what happened. The surgeon asked what was wrong and I explained my thoughts. Then he said the vacuum left by the operation on my enlarged aortic root was filling with sweat. He prescribed a course of anti-inflammatories and assured me I'd be fine. The doctors had been wrong to suggest I'd need a further operation. If they opened me up at all, it would have been for only 10 minutes.

That was all I needed. The surgeon was the first person to tell me I'd be alright and I burst into tears with relief and shook his hand to thank him. I also thanked Martha for her help in making that happen.

I spent a further 10 days or so in hospital, building myself up for being discharged. For Mum and my girlfriend the thought of bringing me back home was a cause for celebration. For some reason, I didn't feel the same way. I was still in a state of depression. Looking back, I'd say that I'd been over hospitalised, if that's the right phrase.

Bringing myself to smile and laugh was very hard. I still felt tender and numb. None of this was very easy for the two people who had waited such a long time for me.

Covid was still happening and media, including the BBC, Sky and TalkSport, contacted me to find out how I was progressing after my operation. I was pleased to talk but inside I wasn't settled. I could feel the valve and every heartbeat. I was so conscious and self-aware and felt I was existing rather than living. I was also struggling to speak clearly after an incident in the hospital when they inadvertently clipped my vocal cords.

I realised how difficult it was for Mum and my girlfriend because I wasn't helping myself and had given up hope. Now I didn't have playing football as a motivation to drive me forward. The best I could look forward to was physically going back into the club. I was lucky I still had a year left on my contract. Although I couldn't play and had no specific role at Newport County, at least I didn't have to worry about money for 12 months.

I went back into the club at the end of July or early August. It was pre-season after our League Two campaign had been abandoned and we were preparing for a restart in 2020/21. I was warmly welcomed back by players and staff which was nice, but I still wasn't being kind to myself.

This was due to a combination of post-traumatic stress and what we were all going through in the world. Everybody found Covid times hard and, in my view, everyone suffered and lost something as a result. Indeed, many are still struggling to recover from those losses today.

In my case, Covid, not the condition itself but what it caused, delayed my recovery. Of the virus itself, I have tested positive a couple of times and had what I'd describe as a flu-like illness. Altogether it made it harder mentally to get myself together and take steps towards a brighter future.

Among the Newport staff who helped me were physio, Tom Gittoes, club doctor David Vaughan, and sports scientist Lewis Binns. They supported me and assured me that my heart was ok. However, I was becoming fixated with it and, as I've said, existing rather than living.

This was the start of what became very bad panic attacks. I'd suffered anxiety before but nothing on this scale. One night I was sitting watching TV with Mum and my girlfriend when I began to feel dizzy. I could feel my heart race and thought something was badly wrong. Now I realise that I was in what they call fight or flight mode when the body is hyperalert. Around this time, I thought only medical people could save me. So, we agreed to ring 999 and the paramedics arrived. They reassured me that nothing was wrong with my heart and started to calm me down.

Unless you've experienced a panic attack, it's difficult to put yourself in my shoes. And until I realised this was a panic attack, I didn't have the context to know what was happening to me. I was thinking irrationally and this was having a negative effect on my body. I didn't seem to have the power to feel safe within myself. I needed someone else – in this case medical staff – to save me.

I also had faith in staff at the football club. I needed to have a purpose and to see the way forward. It seemed logical to me that my future lay within football in some way. Although I didn't have a defined role, they made me feel part of the background staff, even giving me a tracksuit. In addition, I was given a fitness programme consisting of walking and jogging.

At this stage, I felt unsafe and panic-stricken at the thought of going shopping at Morrisons but was fine with being with 25 of the football lads on a bus. For some reason, they made me feel safe.

Another opportunity opened up because of the strange nature of football when it resumed with matches being played behind closed doors. Clubs put more emphasis on providing their own commentaries and I was asked to do co-commentary. This was something new, but I soon began to enjoy it. Games came thick and fast and I started to feel myself again. On the other hand, I'd sometimes go into the changing room for a lie down if things became too much. I was still getting used to the heart valve, my heart racing and dizzy spells.

I forced myself to go to football, but whilst away from the club I still struggled badly. Sitting on the sofa at home, I had a massive panic attack that led me to being taken into hospital. Four doctors told me I was ok, but the important thing was I didn't feel ok. For three weeks afterwards, I didn't feel safe enough to sit in the living room because I associated it with the panic attack. Instead, I'd go to the football club, return home and go to bed – the only other place I felt safe.

Dad kept phoning to try to help, but I was getting worse and worse. Then I had a panic attack in bed. It was at midnight and Mum phoned the ambulance. I asked her to ring Matty Dolan and he lay in bed with me, held my hand and told me I'd be alright.

They wouldn't allow Mum into the hospital, but I phoned David Pipe and he knew somebody at the hospital who helped us get round it. Everybody close to me were sticking together and doing all they could. They say that when you're at your lowest point, you discover who is really there for you and who isn't. And that was the case with me. I will never forget those who supported me when I needed it most.

My mind played tricks on me. I switched to trying to sleep on the sofa but struggled to get any rest. As in hospital, I was fearful if I nodded off, I wouldn't wake up again.

I was speaking with doctors and confiding in people at the football club but neglecting my relationship with my girlfriend. I don't know why. I couldn't control how I was feeling and we were arguing a lot and not in a good place. I realised me being so unwell was making her feel bad – and I didn't like that. We spoke about me getting better, but I couldn't give her a timescale because I didn't know the answer myself.

We'd been together for about 10 or 11 months when we decided to go our separate ways. That wasn't an easy thing to do. I will always be grateful for the help she gave Mum and me at such a terrible time in my life. Yet it seemed I'd been dealt certain cards in life and she had been dealt others. She was on a different path and I couldn't hold her back. I didn't want her to struggle any more. There were times afterwards when I wondered if we made the right decision, but she has been able to move on in her life which is good.

I was constantly seeking more and more reassurance that my heart was ok. I thank the club doctor at Newport that he listened to my chest and told me that I was fine. But I was getting addicted to having to be reassured. The doctor asked if I'd thought about counselling – it would be perfect for me, he said. And he was right. I contacted Sporting Chance through the PFA, and they got me a counsellor. I would recommend it to anyone as counselling helped me to understand more about myself.

During counselling, I was able to speak openly. It's often easier to do so to somebody you don't know. I spoke about the whole shitstorm – retiring from football, open heart surgery, the lot. Breaking things down helped me to see things more clearly.

The counsellor explained that I was still going through trauma – post traumatic stress, if you like. He advised me to be easier on myself – to give myself credit for going through what I had. I started to realise that my recovery wouldn't happen overnight. All I could do was take small steps in the right direction.

Counselling was new to me in several ways. It enabled me to speak freely about myself and without embarrassment. There's a perception out there that counselling is for the weak and you're failing if you need help – nothing could be further from the truth. It takes strength to realise that something is wrong and to confront the issues. At the same time, it was important for me to realise counselling wasn't the complete answer. I had a void in my life that needed filling after the end of my playing career and counselling, however good, was never going to do that.

I took another step forward through becoming aware of a podcast about life after football by former golfer Lewis Harrington and former footballer Dean Hammond. Lewis reached out to me because he could see that I was struggling and arranged to phone me for a chat. I needed someone who understood what I was going through as a recently retired sportsman. The counsellor sympathised from a human and professional point of view but didn't really understand because he had never been in my shoes.

These two shared my grief because they were on the same journey. I no longer felt so alone after speaking with them. They were real too. Things would not get any easier over the next few weeks, they said, I was on a painful path and needed to recognise and understand that.

Lewis said the biggest adjustment that I needed to make was acceptance. In my head I was still fighting what had happened. I hadn't accepted finishing football and the traumatic fashion in which it happened. Lewis told me that I hadn't changed. I may no longer be Mark O'Brien, the footballer, but I was and always had been Mark O'Brien, full stop. I was still me!

Everything I'd projected onto football was really me. I'd seen myself as being strong, tough, never giving in and a leader on the football field and not necessarily the same in the rest of my life. That was wrong. I wasn't given those qualities by football; I gave those qualities to the game. I was and am a strong person outside of sport. This was another light bulb moment when I recognised something I'd never realised before and yet had been staring me in the face all along.

*****

By MATTY DOLAN, Hartlepool and former Newport County footballer and close friend

WHEN I joined Newport, OB was vice captain and we got on straightaway and clicked. As a player, he was 'heart on sleeve'. Much of what we achieved – and I think we overachieved at Newport – was down to us keeping clean sheets and OB was a big part of that. In addition, he led us out at Wembley in the play off final and scored two goals against Oldham (two of very few!).

The FA Cup games were great experiences. Looking at the teamsheet when we played Manchester City, you just had to laugh. Nothing can prepare you for coming up against a team like that, but we knuckled down and were one of very few sides to keep them out for 45 minutes.

It was typical of Mark when he took that Wembley defeat on himself. He was ridiculously unlucky to get that first yellow card – but he's stubborn and it didn't matter how many times we told him that it wasn't his fault.

He has been through so much that you could call him Mr Adversity, but it was a big shock to us all when his heart diagnosis was made (although, as a mate, I knew what happened to him as a teenager).

Footballers put their bodies on the line, but Mark literally put himself on the line every season he played, not knowing if it would be his last.

When he was in hospital, the players clubbed together their Christmas party money to buy him an iPad and Nintendo – he was our skipper and respected within the group.

After the surgery, he went through very difficult times. I knew something about anxiety as my fiancée Chloe is a cognitive behavioural therapist and we had lots of chats with him and tried to help. He also spent time living with us and became part of the family.

Today it's great to see OB in such a good place, both with the club and being happy and enjoying his life. He's found the perfect role at Newport and part of that is because of all he has experienced. In his liaison job and as a co-commentator (I've listened and he's good), he tells it as it is which is typical of him.

Mark is godfather to my boy Oliver and the apple of my daughter Isabella's eye. I'm now at Hartlepool, my hometown club, but we're in contact pretty much every day and, yes, friends for life.

*****

I will also add that for a while I took antidepressants. They helped take the edge off my anxiety at an important time. Depression and anxiety go together and I needed to break the cycle.

It was good for me that at this stage I let people into my life at my darkest time, rather than try to do it all myself. I was interviewed on ITV Wales about my health anxiety – another turning point. I'd got used to speaking to media both during my playing career and afterwards as a co-commentator, but this was different. There I'd been talking about football and was in my comfort zone. Although I'd spoken with a counsellor and friends and colleagues about myself and my health, this was a challenge to speak openly to the world. It felt alien to me, a step into the unknown. Yet doing so has now begun to open so many doors for me and I'd like to think not only helped me but others.

The interviewer told me afterwards that this was one of the bravest things he had ever seen. That gave me back my sense of purpose for the first time since playing football. I could see my story meant something: people would say 'if he can do, so can I'. Today I want to give hope to people who are afraid, so they will not give up on themselves.

My first season after quitting playing was proving a good one for the club. Again, we made cup history, this time in the League Cup. Our 3-1 success over Championship club Watford meant we reached round four for the first time. And we gave Premier League Newcastle United a proper scare by drawing 1-1 before going out agonisingly in the penalty shootout.

Towards the end of the season, Newport again made the

play offs, and I was acting as part of the background staff. Still my anxiety was off the scale. Having seen us beat Forest Green Rovers 2-0 at home in the first leg of the semi-final, I struggled watching the return game after the home side scored two early goals. I could feel my heartbeat and that sense of panic. So, I took myself away from my seat and watched the rest of the game on a screen in the team bus. Fortunately, things improved on the pitch as we battled back to get into the final after a thrilling 4-3 defeat. I think my body struggled to cope with a surge of adrenalin from a tense situation.

Coming home, I was exhausted as if I'd kicked and headed every ball. After that experience, there was no way I was going to Wembley for the final. I argued with Mum who insisted that I was. The turning point was when Newport chairman Gavin Foxhall texted me to say that the club needed a representative to speak in the hospitality boxes and do interviews. Jim Bentley was doing the job for Morecambe, would I do so for Newport?

This gave me an added purpose to go to the game. I bought myself a new three-piece suit and was suited and booted for the big occasion. I stayed in the hotel with the lads and was at the ground about two hours before kick off where I did an interview with Sky Sports. Both this and the hospitality talks went very well and I enjoyed myself.

When we went for our pre-match meal, there were surreal moments that could only happen with Newport. I found myself with Wilfred Bony, the former Swansea City striker who spent various spells training at Newport; and former Arsenal and France legend, Thierry Henry, who became friends with Flynny whilst they did their coaching badges.

I didn't feel anxious doing my job but must admit that did happen during the game. We were still well in the tie with no goals after 90 minutes, but fate was about to strike again.

After the controversy of my dismissal in the Tranmere final, this was a tale of two penalty decisions by referee Bobby Madley, both of which went against us. Early in the game, their goalkeeper came out to try to punch the ball, missed completely and smashed Scot Bennett. In any other circumstance that's got to be a foul and therefore a penalty but, for some reason, the referee was unmoved. To make things worse, Morecambe's winner after 107 minutes came from a penalty I don't think should have been given. Ryan Haynes gave John O'Sullivan a nudge as he ran towards the 18-yard box, but he was on the edge of the D and therefore not in the area.

The whole day exhausted me physically and mentally, but I had the satisfaction, despite the disappointing result, that I'd pushed myself for the first time and achieved what I'd set out to do.

Importantly, I still felt part of the team with Matty Dolan becoming more like a brother and close friendships continuing with Joss Labadie, David Pipe and Mickey Demetriou. Returning to the club before the start of the 2020-21 season, I was given an ambassadorial role which I was delighted with. I had wanted to stay in football, but had no desire to go into either coaching or management. This role enabled me to stay involved.

I was also keen to share my life story with others and was thinking about keynote speaking. Jamille Matt, whom I'd stayed in touch with after he left Newport, advised me to set up a LinkedIn account and, through this, I contacted former Norwich City and Northern Ireland footballer Paul McVeigh, who had become a keynote speaker. We arranged a Zoom call during which I explained my situation. Paul said he was looking for potential speakers whose stories resonated with other people and mine fitted the bill. He ran a speaker's course called Bespoke Elite Speaker Training (BEST) with Leon Lloyd, a former England rugby union international.

I was taking on board Dad's advice to say 'yes' to every opportunity that came my way. BBC invited me to do co-commentary on BBC Wales covering Newport matches and I was also contacted by Ed Daws, of Radio Derby, and covered a few Rams games.

In the New Year, Paul and Leon set up another Zoom call and we had a chat and a laugh before Leon came up with some ideas. They had a course coming up in Manchester in February. It was a very intense five-day event running from 6am to 7pm to train would-be speakers. They then offered support for a full year. This was a commitment on my part but, true to Dad's advice, I decided to go for it. I paid for the course out of my own money because I saw this as the start of a new chapter in my recovery and something outside my comfort zone.

Soon afterwards I had another panic attack. This made me think that I shouldn't attend the course. Public speaking can be stressful. What if I had a panic attack in front of them? I was so close to calling it quits but, no, I wasn't going to give in. I decided to go for it.

I was joined on day one by Paul McVeigh, Leon Lloyd, broadcaster Emily Drake, former Premier League winning footballer Chris Sutton, founder of social enterprise supporting military wives Heledd Kendrick, GB Paralympian Emma Wiggs and Irish rugby union legend Geordan Murphy. I felt young and small beside them. They were much more experienced and had achieved a lot more in their lives, in my view. What was I even doing here?

An actor showed us how to act out your story when speaking. This was the beginning of a few days that opened my eyes and changed my life for the better in many ways. We were all asked to speak for three minutes – one of the hardest three minutes of my life. But, famous or otherwise, we were all in the same boat. It was hard for everyone else as well. I stood there arms folded, giving some of my story before the others provided feedback. They agreed that I had a lot to say and my story was not run-of-the-mill as far as the general public was concerned.

As we had dinner together that evening, I realised that the others all had a success story. My biggest failing is self-doubt and I had to continue to believe that my individual story, failure and trauma included, really mattered.

Each day started at 6am with an ice bath. I'm not going to dress it up – I hated the idea. But it was done to teach us breathing techniques to keep calm on stage. They were still horrible though! This was followed by meditation before we got into the day's activities.

We were taken to a theatre hall and instructed by one of the producers of *Les Miserables*. He spoke about stage presence, including projecting your voice and how to relate to your audience. How to sell your story in other words. Our task later was to speak for six minutes and demonstrate what we had learnt. I tried to act out my story more and maintain better eye contact. One of the things that I liked was the team environment, which I likened to football. We were all in this new challenge together and pulling for each other.

On day three, the ice bath was followed by a visit to a comedy club specially booked out for us. A comedian taught us about introducing humour into our talk. Sometimes a piece of humour or a joke in the right place can bring your audience onto the same playing field as you. Emily spoke on the fourth day about marketing and being your own brand before we tackled a 12-minute talk complete with slides and video. I was able to script my own life and it seemed like a meaningful story.

Then, on day five, we were on a big stage in the auditorium with 100 people dotted around listening. This time the talk was 18 minutes long as we put into practice all that we had learnt during the week. We were beginning to realise how far we had come since that nerve wracking three minutes on day one.

At one point I lost what I was trying to say, but I was experiencing a buzz and excitement that I'd lacked for so long. It gave me an adrenalin rush and feeling of acceptance and achievement like completing pre-season training. I could now see myself getting my life back and finding purpose in what had happened to me. And I'd so nearly talked myself out of attending!

The demons, however, were still there and, a couple of weeks later, I had a panic attack at midnight whilst alone in bed. I phoned Matty Dolan and once again he was great. I packed a bag and went to stay with him and his fiancée at his house for two weeks. I told them that I didn't want the rest of my life to be like this, lurching from one panic attack to another.

But things had begun to shift. This time, I got through without medical support and was soon doing things that showed I was making progress. In the summer, I went back home to Dublin for a few weeks. This meant packing a bag and getting on a plane by myself – things others take for granted but big steps for a man who'd been too scared to step inside Morrisons. I was getting stronger.

CHAPTER NINE
COMING BACK TO ME

By former Newport County physio, TOM GITTOES

I FIRST met Mark a week before his second open heart surgery, having known of him as the no-nonsense centre half who scored the unbelievable goal against the Notts County side that I worked for to keep Newport in the Football League.

At first, he was confident, positive, almost blasé, considering that he was facing life-saving surgery and the end of his playing career. We knew that because Mark was being fitted with a metallic valve and would need to take medication such as blood thinners, there was no way back on the field for him.

I had never come across a situation like this with a footballer and contacted the NHS two or three weeks later about his rehabilitation to live a healthy life. It was soon clear that he was much more physically capable than others in the same situation and we got him running and doing strengthening work. He was walking and running 5k whilst we continued to monitor his heart rate.

Later we noticed that he started to get fixated about his heart monitor and then one night Mark called saying he couldn't breathe and didn't know what to do. I said this was a job for the paramedics. The same thing happened a couple of weeks later.

I phoned the PFA's specialist counselling team who deal with professional athletes after Mark had another panic attack – more public this time on the training ground. It was becoming clear that he had more than just a physical problem.

Going onto antidepressants and with counselling in place, he began to become more stable, but we weren't out of the woods yet. The panic attacks became more frequent at night until, around two months after surgery, something shifted in Mark's mind. It was then that he started to realise he needed sorting out – and the only person who could do so was Mark himself.

I think it was at the play off final at Wembley where Mark had his speaking and interviewing duties that we saw him come alive again as a person for the first time.

He carved out a new role for himself at Newport whilst James Rowberry was manager, bridging the gap between the gaffer and the players. Although I've since moved on to Swansea City, I saw how good he is. He is superb at guiding young players because he has a wise head on his shoulders. He must tread a fine line in that post but he's the perfect man to do it.

I've been with him in Newport when people have come up and shouted 'hero' at Mark and I know how appropriate that is.

To see where Mark is now in his life after all he has gone through is remarkable.

*****

THE last part of my story is about my recovery – a journey not a destination. I'm still experiencing and living it and will do so as long as I have breath in my body. I'm not there – I haven't made it. But that's the point. For the first time in my life, I'm happy living in the moment, not worrying what lies ahead.

I've already mentioned some of the key people and things that have helped me, such as the support and expertise at the football club, counselling, the public speaking course and finding new outlets after the end of my playing career.

Another positive was not getting too immersed in the news, particularly during the pandemic. After a while, I purposely didn't listen. When my parents rang to say what was happening with Covid – I didn't want to know. I told them that I didn't care – that's not fair, I do care, but I've come to realise that I shouldn't stress about things I can't do anything about. Instead, I now try to stick instead to what I can control.

I've benefitted, too, from people who have come into my life – sometimes the most unexpected people. I've mentioned several of my teammates and the close friendships I've built with them, but when Kevin Ellison walked into the building, my expectations weren't high.

From my playing experience, he was a nightmare, a maverick, immersed in the dark arts – a good striker, if you like. To the fans, he is a hero who brings energy to the game when he walks on the pitch, or the pantomime villain, an opponent easily singled out for abuse. I discovered that, as a person, he is far different. He may not realise it, but he was a big help to me. We had lots of chats together and I found him to be a wise head who is very aware of the importance of mental health. It was like speaking to an older brother and I took on board a lot of his advice.

Today football and Newport County are still very important features of my life.

I was still helping the staff as best I could as the 2021-22 season, the first when crowds returned after Covid, got off to an unsettled start. Once again, we had problems with our ground, meaning that our opening four league fixtures were played away from home.

When we finally played at Rodney Parade we got hammered 8-0 by Premier League Southampton in the EFL Cup after winning 1-0 at Ipswich in round one. After all the brilliant performances we had put in against top sides in recent seasons, this brought us firmly back to earth. This time the history we made wasn't to our liking as it was the biggest away win in Saints' 135-year history.

Michael Flynn sat out that sorry night after testing positive for Covid and a few weeks later he was out of the door altogether. We were in 15th spot after just nine league games and I found it a shock and disappointment to see him go. I had created so many personal memories with him, both during the 'great escape' season for which he will always be fondly remembered at Rodney Parade and afterwards, when we were usually challenging at the other end of League Two.

A local lad and former player, Flynn was a prime character in putting 'the Newport' back into Newport and building us up as the underdogs and battlers who never knew when we were beaten. I'd also like to thank him personally for all the encouragement and support that he gave me after my operation, making me feel very welcome at the club even though I could no longer contribute on the pitch. He is another reason that my recovery is now going really well.

Wayne Hatswell stayed on as we searched for a new first team manager, which gave the club and me some continuity, but naturally I was concerned about how this was going to affect me. My contract had officially run out at the end of the 2020/21 season and there was no guarantee the new boss would want me around.

That new man was James Rowberry, who had been Cardiff City's under 21 coach. I did what I could to impress the new manager although, in my case where I was helping with personal issues, that wasn't easy. I couldn't invent problems to solve, so I went about my business much as before.

James brought in his own coaching staff and impressed me with his vision. He was looking to expand the club in all areas, from our general professionalism to the playing style. He thought that Newport County after two play off final defeats needed to go to the next step and he was the right man to do it. Fair enough.

He also took time to look at my input and find out for himself what I was like around the place. From this came the next step in my journey. James looked at what I was doing with the coaches, the academy lads and the analysts and made the player care role, which I'd kind of dropped into over the months, official. This was a big help because I was getting paid again and had a purpose.

The role is becoming more common at clubs these days but can be more linked with the academy. In our case, I am a go-between linking the manager with the players. It's a job that requires a lot of trust and one I feel my experiences – even the negative ones – have prepared me very well for. For example, I can relate to a young player struggling to get himself back onto the field through injury because I have been in that situation and know how it feels. I know it's not purely a physical challenge, but also a mental one. I recognise how lonely it can feel with the temptation on bad days to think that it's never going to happen.

Players go through all sorts of problems that fans, even managers, know little about when they are performing below their best on the pitch. I've encountered a fair few myself. Often the last person whom they wish to speak with is the manager for fear, perhaps, they will be viewed as weak. On other occasions, they really need to talk to the boss because he is the best person to help.

My role involves judging if the player's issue is something that the manager needs to know about. If it's better for player and club the issue is kept between us, I maintain confidentiality. When I think that the manager needs to know, I ask the player if it's ok for me to share it with him.

Players aren't always up front with their issues and sometimes it can be the wrong time to speak with them. I look for tell-tale signs of a player not looking themselves, perhaps being quieter than usual.

I will quote a very good example of striker Dom Telford, who was struggling to get into the side under Michael Flynn and was on the verge of a move to National League side AFC Fylde. The truth was the manager, for whatever reason, didn't fancy him and he couldn't see a pathway back into our side. I saw that he was looking down in training, so took the chance to speak with him one-to-one. I said that he was one of the best finishers at Newport County but, for now, needed to ignore everything else and train for himself.

It's strange how things work in football. Things can change very quickly with unexpected opportunities coming out of the blue. Dom needed to be in the right place to take that chance if it came along.

Instead of dropping down a division, which he didn't really want to do, he began to knuckle down and was brought back into the side when James Rowberry took over. That's no criticism of Flynny; football is all about opinions and the new boss obviously liked what he saw.

In Rowberry's more possession-based side, Dom topped our goalscoring charts with 25 in the league and 26 in all competitions. He came up to me at the end of the season and thanked me personally. I asked 'what for?' and he said I'd been probably the only person at the club who still believed in him and that had given him a lift.

He called me his hero and I returned the compliment. Watching Dom smashing in those goals, there was an extra smile on my face. I was particularly pleased for one of the nicest lads in football. Since then, Dom has got his big money move to Crawley Town and I wish him all the best.

My working day begins at 8.30am when I join the manager and other staff for a meeting. We talk about the day and the week ahead. I take my place on the training ground, putting out the cones, taking part in passing drills and generally helping before the day ends between 3pm and 3.30pm.

Match days bring a different routine. For a traditional Saturday 3pm kick off, I report to Rodney Parade at about 12.30pm. The team is announced on the Friday and I organise the lads who haven't made the side to carry out duties, such as signing autographs and going around the executive boxes.

The players get there between 1.30pm and 1.45pm as attention turns to the match. Unless I'm on commentary duty, I sit in the dugout to watch. This gives me a good view of what is going on. I'm not part of the coaching staff but, when the lads come over for a drink, I often have a word or two to encourage them. The manager knows that I'm there when needed.

Sometimes I see a player's reaction when they are taken off and know they aren't in the best of moods. This is a time just to take note because the last thing they want is to talk. I allow them to sulk but ensure I'm there for them during the week.

To a young player, getting substituted can seem like the end of the world, particularly if they've waited a while to get their chance. As a more experienced footballer, I share with them that the game changes from week to week. I've been left out of the side many times and fought my way back in. But that's more likely to happen if you show a good attitude in training and are willing to learn from your mistakes.

Not all players want my help. Individuals have their own agendas. In fact, I'd argue today that it is becoming a much more individual game – unfortunately. But that's fine. I need to be sensitive to the needs and ways of individuals. Some need an arm around their shoulder and a timely word of encouragement; others a verbal boot up the arse. It's my job to critique what is going on rather than be everyone's best mate. If I think someone needs to improve, I tell them.

I adopt the same principle when I'm co-commentating – a

job that I have come to love. It's very good of the club to allow me to combine my staff role with working with Rob Phillips of BBC Radio Wales. Rob was the first to hug me when I went down the tunnel after scoring that goal against Notts County and we get on very well. But, as he knows, my role comes with responsibilities and that is sometimes a delicate balancing act.

Listeners want to hear the game from a Newport point of view, but I try to tell it as it is, rather than give a biased impression. That can mean pointing out mistakes and failings among the players, but I try to do so with integrity. If I wouldn't say the same thing to a player's face, I won't say it on the radio.

There's been a further change at the top with James Rowberry being dismissed after 13 games of the 2022-23 season and being replaced by Graham Coughlan. I had a lot of time for James, not least because he was so helpful to me. I could see what he wanted to do with his possession-based football, but also that it was never going to be easy to achieve.

Change doesn't happen overnight and it was always going to take hard work and effort to implement James' plan more effectively. We'd thrived on clean sheets and keeping games tight and changing that template was difficult. I recognised James Rowberry as an outstanding and very promising coach – the youngest ever at 29 to get his UEFA pro licence. But I don't think that his methods were best suited to League Two. Given the chance, I believe that he would do better at a higher level. Managers get very little time today. James was very much about player development and that's more suited to being coach of an under 21 side than a manager.

He didn't do badly in 2021-22 as we finished the season in 11th spot and was confident that with marquee signing Omar Bogle leading the line and new signings, Sam Bowen, James Waite, Declan Drysdale and Offrande Zanzala, who was in Derby's academy when I was in the first team, we would go on to bigger and better things.

James filled everyone with confidence and was very meticulous about his work, so we began the 2022-23 with optimism. He was looking for perfection from the lads, but nothing is ever perfect at Newport. The team played well on occasions but was inconsistent. In my view, he concentrated too much on the opposition with his team selections, rather than what we could do. For example, he picked a more physical line up to face Stevenage and a technically more adapt side against Stockport. Rotating the team is very fashionable in modern times but it's also important to build relationships.

The job proved to be a big learning curve for him, perhaps a case of too much too soon, but hopefully one that he will learn from. His aim to make Newport County into a better club had to be admired and he remains an amazing coach.

I will add here that James had his own heart issue as in the summer of 2022 a routine check-up showed that he had a third-degree atrioventricular heart block and he was fitted with a pacemaker. Naturally we wish him well.

James leaving meant that I was left wondering what next for me? Would I be seen by the new boss as Flynn or even Rowberry's man? Being without a leader for a couple of games was worrying particularly as we were too close for comfort to the bottom two. The 'R' word had not been spoken about at Newport since our great escape and fortunately, this was only a minor flirtation.

Football is a rollercoaster, but I believe Newport, as I'm writing, are back in good shape. Following our wobble at the start of the 2022-23 season, we finished the campaign in 15th place. And my personal fears again proved without foundation. The first plus point was when I realised that Graham was from Dublin. More than that he used to play for Cherry Orchard and his family home was only 20 minutes from mine. That gave me encouragement that we would find common ground.

From the moment he walked through the door, I could see that aura of a manager. It's difficult to put into words but I recognised the same sense of authority that I found in Nigel Clough and Stuart McCall, guys who demand instant respect. He sat down and talked with staff and it was clear he had ambition and wanted all of his colleagues to have the same. He challenged all of us to be better at what we do and to set our sights high.

The Irish connection was added to when Coughlan brought in another Dubliner Joe Dunn, his assistant at Mansfield as his number two. Joe is someone I knew as a manager and together with the Coughlan has bought into the club and taken Newport to his heart. In their first few months, they have worked towards restoring Rodney Parade as a fortress and reverting to what we were good at – competing and keeping clean sheets.

The manager is seeking to produce 'winning football' – if the ball must go long, play it long; yes, we'd love to play attractive football but we're not going to turn overnight into a Manchester City. Good loan signings such as Callum Kavanagh, Charlie McNeil and Matt Baker came in and we improved without doing as well as the management team demanded. I know they were disappointed that we failed to win on the final day when we could have finished three places higher. I believe they are the right men for the club and that when we kick off again, we will continue to improve.

As for me, I've learnt to accept where I am in all aspects of life. I'm ambitious because I want to make a difference and make what I have gone through worthwhile. But I don't set myself targets of where I want to be in the future.

I have become more aware, through circumstances that I would never have chosen to go through. I know more about myself and life itself. I can even go as far as to say that I'm grateful for all of my experiences because they have made me the man I am today.

One of many realisations is that I'm still a young man. I will be 31 years old in November 2023. Footballers and young folk who play other sports often feel they are 'getting old' or are 'finished' because most end their playing careers in their early 30s. That creates a psychological obstacle towards going forward. We need to realise that we have most of our lives still in front of us and we are still the same person.

I've already described that I subconsciously at least used to separate Mark O'Brien, the footballer, from Mark O'Brien, the human being. Put me on a football pitch and my courage knew no bounds. That was what my first professional manager, Nigel Clough, first noticed about me and was talked about throughout my career. It took me to go through counselling however to realise that those qualities are mine and I am free to use them in other areas of my life.

In recent months, I have taken strides forward by improving

my fitness. I felt that, having got through my period of crisis, my physical appearance wasn't what I wanted it to be. Understandably perhaps, after finishing football early, I slipped into a comfort zone of eating what I wanted and had more than reversed that loss of weight in hospital. I had been 11 stone 7lb but was around 14 stones and feeling sluggish.

So, I reached out again for specialist help as I needed more than a personal trainer. I hadn't been in touch with Kevin Hendrick, Jeff's brother, for some time but knew he ran an online fitness training programme. He wrote back to set up a video call. I'd been scared about how hard I could push myself because of my heart condition and there were still 'what ifs?' in my mind.

I was looking for someone who was not only good but had some knowledge of what I had gone through. I trusted Kevin as I'd known him for a long time and he had my best interests at heart. He thought that he could help and put me on a four-week programme that would make a difference. I recognised that he was speaking with me as a counsellor as much as a personal trainer.

I sent him photos of myself from all angles to highlight what he was dealing with. His advice was that because I had been a professional athlete until recently, I should tackle the four-week plan at my own pace. Just make sure you do it at some time during the day, he said. He also gave me a diet plan. It was better not to have someone pushing me as that would have made me feel uncomfortable.

I started going to a local gym in Newport. The sessions lasted about an hour to 75 minutes and involved upper body work and lifting weights. I'm not allowed to lift heavy weights because of my condition, but my body has now become accustomed to me increasing the weights. My diet has changed to eating the right foods and cutting down on calories. I now eat smaller meals four or five times a day. This gets my metabolism working better and I was soon feeling myself again.

After four weeks I was beginning to enjoy myself. Kevin was always there for me. He asked me to send new photographs and, comparing them with the first ones, we could see the difference straightaway. I had lost a couple of kilograms and was very happy to carry on. I still had a nagging worry about doing too much but Kevin made things easy. Working with his guidance made me feel like a player again, being in a position of trust with a member of staff. I gave him a lot of credit for filling me with confidence and showing me what I am still capable of. After another four weeks, I'd lost another kilogram and my body shape was improving with less fat.

My weight had come down between five and six kg in ten weeks and Kevin said that I was doing brilliantly and asked where I wanted to take this. I said I wanted to get physically stronger and better by adding more calories. I also did extra training, concentrating on my chest, arms, legs and shoulders. I thanked him for everything and he said I was the one putting in all the work – all he was doing was to write out the plan. There was mutual respect between us and I could see that this was the next chapter in my recovery.

Understandably there were times when I struggled to get to the gym because life got in the way, and he told me not to beat myself up about it but to do it the following day. I felt I was letting him down when this happened, but he reassured me that wasn't so. He emphasised that, once again, this was a long process. "You are not building for tomorrow, you are building for your future," he said.

Today I go to the gym about five days a week for about an hour to an hour and a half. The result has been that I have fallen back in love with fitness, discarding my worries, excuses and 'what ifs?'.

I have learnt that the mind rather than the body is the biggest battleground as with other areas of life. Once I get my mental state right, I can tell my body what to do. When you work on yourself, your body must follow. We have spoken much about the power of the mind. The more I work with him, the more I understand what is good and not good for me.

I still have my limitations. I am on blood thinners and blood pressure tablets and ensure that I am comfortable with what I am doing. If I don't like something, I stop and find an alternative.

Altogether my gym work has been about far more than improving my physical appearance or making me feel better. It's been the next stage on my learning journey. For so long, my mind controlled me. I worried about the next football match, the next challenge in my life and, ultimately, if I'd be able to take my next breath. Taking control of my mind is changing all that. Yes, I have my wobbles, my 'what ifs?' and moments of panic but overall I am now much more mentally stronger than I've ever been.

I no longer think of my life as tragic or unlucky. I am thankful for what I can do and have, rather than begrudging what I can't. I could have played 600 Football League games had I steered largely clear of injuries and not had a heart condition. But I'm grateful that I played just over 200 games in the league and cup competitions.

Why? Because that's what happened and there's nothing I nor anyone else could have done to change it. I created memories that will last forever – leading my team out at Wembley, scoring THAT goal that made me into an instant local hero, running out at Nottingham where the odds were so stacked against us and watching my mate score the winning goal, playing at Celtic Park, the scene of my early football dreams.

Nobody can take any of that away. And yet, save for fate, none of it could have happened. I could have been one of those young lads – not privileged to have been part of an elite football club where medical care and expertise was on hand – to drop dead due to an undiagnosed heart condition. So, yes, I was lucky, blessed even, to do what I did.

I have special, special people in my family and in my life, as well as friends. People who have been tested to the very limits by what has happened to me but come through every time. When I needed them, they have been there for me. When I learnt sufficiently about life to reach out for help, I have discovered others with abilities and care that I sometimes didn't know they had.

So now I am thankful for the small things in life – waking up in the morning, having breakfast, knowing that the whole day is in front of me and I can often do as I wish. The 'small' things are the most important, the 'big' ones pure bonuses!

I continue to take on board Dad's advice to say 'yes' to everything within reason. What's the worst that can happen? I may find I've made a wrong turning, so I'll turn back. But by being open minded and saying 'yes' I am again experiencing so much. Examples include speaking in schools in front of students about mental health, sharing my story with Sporting Chance, helping the British Heart Foundation and speaking with fans' groups in Derby and Newport.

Every time I say 'yes' I open the door to creating more memories and that's what life is all about. When I am older, I will reflect on the incredible things that I have seen and done. It won't be about winning and losing – being there and competing is success enough.

After speaking at a question and answer session in Derby for Rams' fan Blake Fallows, someone got in touch with him and said they wanted to see me. It was through that contact that I was introduced to former Leicester City chief executive and now director of Morgan Lawrence Barrie Pierpoint and that's how you are reading this today.

It was Dad who first suggested that I should write a book. "Why me?" I replied. "I'm not a big name." "Everything you have gone through in your life is one big story," he said. And, as usual, he was right. The time had now come to put my thoughts and experiences into print.

I think you'll agree that it's been more than just a football story. I have shared this because I don't want any of what has happened to me to be wasted. If just one young person gains hope and thinks 'if he can go through all that and be fine, I will never give up' that's good enough for me.

In these very difficult times, mental health is an issue like never before. My message is that you can come through and win the battle of the mind.

It won't be easy and it won't be instant, but you can come to enjoy life like you never done before.

Statistics

	Appearances	Goals
Derby County 2008—2015	35	0
Motherwell (loan) 2014—2015	21	0
Luton Town 2015—2016	9	0
Southport (loan) 2015—2016	12	1
Newport County 2016—2020	127	3
Total	**204**	**3**

Represented Republic of Ireland at under 16, under 17 and under 19 level.

Honours

Republic of Ireland - Under 16 Player of Year	Winner	2009
Derby County - Academy Player of the Year	Winner	2009
Newport County - League Two Play Off Final	Runners Up	2019

ACKNOWLEDGEMENTS

I'd like to thank:

Mam, Dad and my brother James .
Thomas 'spud" Murphy, Mark O'Brien (Derby scout), Jeff
Hendrick, Elliot Coles, Jonny Doram, Daire Smith, Kevin
Hendrick, Joss Labadie, Matty Dolan, Mike Flynn & Wayne
Hatswell, Mickey Demetriou, Nigel Clough, James Rowberry,
Graham Coughlan, Joe Dunne, Jamille Matt, Joe Day, Leon
Llyod, Paul McVeigh, Emma Wiggs, Heledd Kendrick, Emily
Drake, Chris Sutton, Geordan Murphy, Daniel Vaughan, Lewis
Binns, Thomas Gittoes, Neil Sullivan, Steve Haines, Simon
Parselle, Gary Sweet, Blake Fallows.
My publishers Morgan Lawrence: Mathew Mann, Barrie
Pierpoint, Holly Mann, Lois Hide, Lee Clark, Harry Worgan.
My ghostwriter John Brindley.
Nicola Johns, the Newport County photographer.
Julia Unwin, the Southport FC photographer.
Andy Clarke, the Derby County photographer.
David and Harry Essam for supporting the prodution of this
book.
Everyone at Glenfield hospital.
Everyone at Derby County & Newport County.
The supporters of every club I have played for.
Finally, all my friends and family back home.

Mark

MORGAN LAWRENCE
PUBLISHING SERVICES

The following books are available to purchase from Morgan Lawrence and all major book retailers

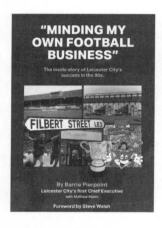

"MINDING MY OWN FOOTBALL BUSINESS"

The inside story of Leicester City's success in the 90s.

FILBERT STREET LE2

By Barrie Pierpoint
Leicester City's first Chief Executive
with Mathew Mann

Foreword by Steve Walsh

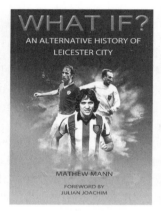

WHAT IF?
AN ALTERNATIVE HISTORY OF LEICESTER CITY

MATHEW MANN

FOREWORD BY
JULIAN JOACHIM

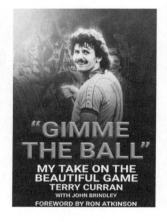

"GIMME THE BALL"
MY TAKE ON THE BEAUTIFUL GAME
TERRY CURRAN
WITH JOHN BRINDLEY
FOREWORD BY RON ATKINSON

JULIAN JOACHIM

My Life In Football
YOU MUST BE JOACHIM

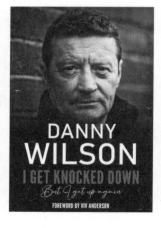

DANNY WILSON
I GET KNOCKED DOWN
But I get up again
FOREWORD BY VIV ANDERSON

THE SEAGULLS BEST EVER SEASON

The incredible story of Brighton's 2022-23 season

TONY NOBLE
FOREWORD BY JOHNNY CANTOR

Email: hello@morganlawrence.co.uk
www.morganlawrence.co.uk

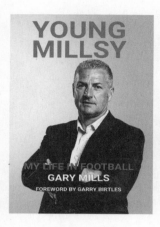

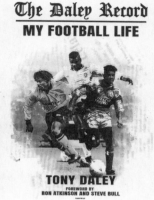

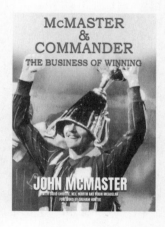